An Ongoing Affair

Turkey & I

Book I: The Bereketli Years, 1964-1966

Heath W. Lowry

© Çitlembik / Nettleberry Publications, 2008
© Heath W. Lowry, 2008

First printing, September 2008

Library of Congress Cataloging-in-Publication Data

W. Lowry, Heath.
    An Ongoing Affair-Turkey and I: the Bereketli years 1964-1966/Heath W. Lowry.-
Istanbul: Çitlembik Publications, 2008.
197 p.: 20 photo; 14x21 cm
ISBN: 978-9944-424-53-0

1. Autobiography
2. Bereketli (Turkey)--Social life and customs

I. Title.
II. The Bereketli years 1964-1966

LC:CT25.L69 2008   DC: 808.06692

Editor: Rebecca Erol
Cover Design and Layout: Çiğdem Dilbaz

Printed at Ayhan Matbaası
Mahmutbey Mah. Deve Kaldırım Cad.
Gelincik Sokak No.: 6 Kat: 3
Bağcılar, İstanbul
Tel: (+90 212) 445 05 63

In Turkey:
Şehbender Sokak 18/4
Asmalımescit - Tünel
34430 Istanbul
www.citlembik.com.tr

In the USA:
Nettleberry LLC
44030 123rd St.
Eden, South Dakota 57232
www.nettleberry.com

To Letitia
In Friendship
[signature]

An Ongoing Affair

Turkey & I

Book I: The Bereketli Years, 1964-1966

Heath W. Lowry

Çitlembik Publications 154

CONTENTS

FOREWORD

Over four decades ago, when a young man of twenty-one, I embarked on what was to become the most formative experience of my life. The events I encountered between October 1964 and March 1966, while living in a remote mountain village in northwestern Turkey have never left me, and, indeed, in one sense, the village of Bereketli ('Blessedness') has never really let me go. It has taken me forty-four years to come to terms with the significance of the Bereketli years in shaping the course of my life. For it was there that I became a man, just as it was there that what has become my lifelong fascination with Turkey, its people and its history began.

The villagers of Bereketli taught me not only the meaning of *misafirperverlik* (literally the act of caring for or nourishing a guest or visitor), but also instilled in me a sense of fatality, best summed up by the oft-repeated phrase *inşaallah* (if God so wills). By their willingness to share what little they had with a stranger they touched a chord in my heart, just as by their stoicism in accepting whatever came their way, they taught me the futility of thinking that we are ever really in control.

It was the friendship of the *Muhtar* (elected village head) Kâmil Aslantekin that served to guide me through each new experience, and, at the same time, explained what must have often seemed to the villagers to be my rather strange behavior, in such a manner that it too became acceptable. He was the *ağabey* (elder brother) I never had, and his countless acts of kindness turned what otherwise might have been a miserable eighteen months into the most memorable period of my life.

The friendships I made, with young and old alike, remain today some of the closest human encounters I have ever enjoyed. The young unmarried men of the village, known as *delikanlıs* (wild bloods), such as Özcan Can and Turhan Demiralp; married men, such as Mehmet Sadık Demirel, Ayhan Hangül, and Muamber Erdem; the village school teachers, including Mustafa *Hoca* (Mustafa Demiralp, a native of Bereketli who was a product of the Village Institute program); the carpentry and masonry course instructors, Kemal Beyaz and Yusuf (whose last name I no longer recall); and virtually every other man in the village, through their hospitality, their sharing of their home-grown tobacco, their signaling to the proprietors of the village coffee houses that the next glass of tea I drank was to go on their account, and numerous other acts of kindness, made it clear that I was more than a guest; they made me feel at home in Bereketli.

The series of sketches or vignettes that follow are representative of both the high and low points of my Bereketli days. They are subjective recollections, indeed a few may be exaggerated in tone, due to having been told and retold over the intervening forty years. Others are purposely muted, for there are memories that even with the passing of time I still hesitate to recall. With one or two notable exceptions, the chapters all deal with the interactions I had with the men of Bereketli. This is a reflection of the fact that I was living in a male world, whether it was in the coffee house, or hunting in the hills.

That said, this work is humbly dedicated to all the Bereketlians: to the small children who followed *Hit Ağabey* (elder brother Heath) about the village, to the girls and women who smiled and nodded in greeting, to the *delikanlıs* and men (young and old) with whom I spent my waking hours. Most of my Bereketli friends are gone, '*nur içinde yatsınlar*' (may they rest in peace), and even those who were young children when I lived amongst them are today grandparents.

Indeed, it was a growing awareness of my own mortality that, after so many years, finally prompted me to set down on paper the story of my introduction to Turkey. I began by simply jotting down a list of what would ultimately become chapter headings. I did so at the urging of the journalist Rauf Tamer, who had been after me for some time to tell him about my life in Turkey, so that he could then write a book about it. It was only when I had begun to set down the outline of what I planned to share with him that I began writing. What follows is the result; as I recalled those far-off days in Bereketli the words began to flow.

Setting down on paper the recollections of my Bereketli days was for me a cathartic experience. I hope that these vignettes will be of interest too for you, the readers.

INTRODUCTION

As is the case with well over half of the country's urban residents today, my life in Turkey began not in Istanbul, Ankara or Izmir, but rather in a small Anatolian village, that of Bereketli ('Blessedness'), nestled in the foothills of *Kaz Dağ* (Mount Ida) some twenty-five kilometers northwest of Balıkesir. It was only after spending close to two years in that setting that I, as so many millions of other Turkish villagers, was to migrate to the city. For this reason I have always felt a certain affinity, not to mention sympathy, for those millions of Turks who have been transplanted from the relative security of Anatolian village life to the hustle and bustle of Turkey's metropolitan centers. That experience gave me a perspective that those Turks born in the country's cities have never shared.

With this in mind, and after a great deal of urging by friends (who have been regaled over the past forty years by tales of my introduction to the country I have come to love), I decided to set down on paper a series of reminiscences detailing both the high and low points of my Turkish experiences during the first two years of what has become my four-decades-plus ongoing affair with my adopted homeland.

Having spent a rather nomadic childhood (I grew up in south India and spent the two years before coming to Turkey running a bar on the island of Formentera in Spain and living in Tangier, Morocco), in the Spring of 1964, I filled out an application to join what the late president John Kennedy had created three years earlier as the Peace Corps. A few weeks later, having forgotten that I had done so, I was surprised when I opened the mail and found a letter informing me that I had been accepted for a three-month training program to prepare me to serve as a 'Rural Community Development' Peace Corps Volunteer in Turkey. Having recovered from my initial shock, my first reaction was to reach for an atlas to make sure that Turkey was where I thought it was: somewhere east of Western Europe and west of India! I now knew where I was going, even if I didn't have the vaguest idea as to the meaning of 'Rural Community Development,' or for that matter just what the Peace Corps was all about. Nor was I all that sure just what twist of fate had decided that out of the dozens of countries round the world that had opened their doors to the Peace Corps, my spin of the wheel had landed on Turkey.

It was only later that I remembered that when filling out the application form there had been a question with three blank boxes asking that I rank the three countries that I would like to serve in. At that stage of my life I was fixated with islands and quickly filled in the first box with 'Ceylon,' and the second box with 'South Pacific.' As I had no third choice, it was only force of habit that made me decide to write something in the last box, and to this day I am uncertain as to why I wrote 'Middle East.' Whatever my reasoning at the time, as fate would have it, those two words were to determine the future course of my life.

Turkey was still considered part of the Middle East in those days, but because my first choice Ceylon had just elected its first socialist prime minister–a woman whose first action was to change the island's name to Sri Lanka and whose second step was to throw the Peace Corps out of her country–that option was out. As the Peace Corps did not begin to send volunteers to the South Pacific islands for another couple of years, thereby eliminating that possibility as well, my third choice had, by a process of elimination, become my first, and I was poised to take the step that would literally shape the rest of my life.

Three months later, having been subjected to an intensive, and as time would show, generally worthless course of instruction in Turkish, I, with my active vocabulary of under two hundred words, together with sixty-eight other similarly unprepared young Americans, was poised to do my part in helping develop an as yet unnamed Turkish village. We memorized a large number of useless phrases, such as *buralarda benzinci var mı?* (is there a gasoline station round here?) – I say useless because not only were Peace Corps volunteers forbidden to drive in Turkey, but the village I was destined to live in didn't even have a real road. Also, after having listened to countless lectures on life in a Turkish village, some of which were delivered by a volunteer who had just returned from two years in Turkey and the remainder by academics who had never come closer to their subject than the glimpse one got from the windows of a fast-moving bus en route from Ankara to Istanbul, I was given an airplane ticket and told to be at Kennedy Airport in New York a week later.

The vignettes that follow all stem from the unknown urge that prompted me to fill in the blank on the Peace Corps application form with the words 'Middle East.' That choice led me first to the Anatolian village of Bereketli where I was to learn a variety of lessons that have stood me well in the intervening years, leading into a career as an·academic whose research and publications focus on Turkey and her Ottoman past. In the course of the past forty years I have come in contact with all manner of Turks, from village shepherds and fishermen to prime ministers and presidents, from titans of industry to the corner *bakkalçı*s (grocers), and I have learned and continue to learn from all of them. Their countless acts of hospitality and kindness have instilled in me an appreciation for them and their country. I was born an American (a decision I had no choice in), but I have chosen to live my life devoted to Turkey, her people and her history. It has been an odyssey filled with countless encounters and memories, some of which I will share with you in the following pages.

PART I
ARRIVAL IN TURKEY
(October 1964)

Chapter 1

The Otel Berlin and the
Ankara brothels (*genel evleri*)

It was a fourteen-hour trip from New York to Ankara, and Pan Am managed to arrive in Turkey at such an hour that it was not only night, but aside from the dim lights flickering in the terminal, pitch black. The trip had not been a pleasant one as the departure from Kennedy Airport had been preceded by a last visit from our Greek-American Peace Corps doctor who had suddenly remembered that, along with all the inoculations and vaccinations he had already inflicted upon us, he had forgotten the mandatory shot for hepatitis: gamma globulin. This meant that one by one sixty-nine Peace Corps volunteers were ushered into a small side room, ordered to bare their backsides, and, in accordance with their body weights received the mandatory shot (or shots as was the case with me). In those years this particular torture was administered in dosages determined by one's body weight. For me this meant sixteen centiliters – a dosage that was too large for a single syringe, thereby entailing a shot in each cheek. We were all assured that hepatitis was a major problem in Turkey and that this was a necessary preventative. What we were not told was that the half-life of gamma globulin was six weeks, that meant that we were only going to be protected for the first month and a half of what was scheduled to be a twenty-one-month stint in a Turkish village.

Later on, when I had become a bit more familiar with the divide separating Turks and Greeks, I decided that our Greek-American Peace Corps physician had injected us not with a prophylactic, but rather with his own prejudice against our having been (in his opinion) foolish enough to want to spend two years in Turkey. Be that as it may, sixty-nine young Americans, too sore to sit, flew standing up for fourteen hours as Pan American Flight 1 made, what seemed like, its never-ending way to Ankara's Esenboğa Airport.

In 1964 Esenboğa was not yet a suburb of Ankara, nor was it linked to the capital with a six-lane highway. Upon leaving the terminal we were herded onto buses and set off in total darkness for what was to have been our first glimpse of Turkey. Once again, most of us stood for the one-hour trip until, finally, the buses drew up in front of the not-so-imposing *Otel Berlin* in, what later I was to learn was, the Ulus quarter of Ankara.

Too tired and excited to even think of sleep (despite having been up for the previous twenty-four hours), I was determined to explore my new surroundings. I found an equally adventurous companion and, as we were about to set out, we were approached by another Peace Corps volunteer who happened to be staying in the hotel. Having arrived in Turkey three months earlier he was eager to impress us with his newly acquired knowledge and enquired where we were going. When told that we just wanted to get a feel for the city he suggested that we walk down the hill with him so that he could show us a site worth seeing: the Ankara *genel evleri* (literally, 'general houses,' i.e., municipal brothels). As the word '*ev*' (house) was among the two hundred I had committed to memory, along with the plural '*ler*,' I assumed that we were going to someone's house. While I also knew the word '*genel*' (general), I had no idea what it meant when used in conjunction with the word *evler* (houses). As a result, I really had no idea where we were headed. Needless to say, when we arrived at our destination and passed through the barbed wire gate and past the policemen standing guard, I was more than a little surprised. As we wound our way past a steady throng of men, stopping on occasion in front of the houses where the ladies of the night displayed their not-so-appealing wares, I had my first taste of culture shock. In less than twenty-four hours I had been transplanted from the hustle and bustle of downtown Manhattan (where as a parting gift from my native clime I had been issued a ticket for jaywalking) to the back streets of Ankara's seedier side. Fatigued by lack of sleep, compounded by having stood for most of the past fifteen hours, I literally walked about for an hour or so in a state of shock. As I did so, I have a clear recollection of beginning to wonder whether or not my coming to Turkey had been a terrible mistake.

I do not recall leaving the *genel evleri*, but I do know that I had not been tempted to partake of its offerings. On the way back to the hotel, I remember stopping at a restaurant and sampling my first Turkish food. It was a bowl of soup, called *işkembe çorbası,* that reeked of garlic as did our fellow patrons and myself after the first sip. As the word *işkembe* (tripe) had not yet permeated my 200-word vocabulary (but *çorba* had), I only knew that it was soup. Forty-five years later I cannot pass an *işkembeci* without recalling my first night and first meal in Turkey. Fortunately, it was not, in either case, to be my last.

Chapter 2

Ismet Inönü & 'Don't cry, please don't cry, little man'

My first two days in Turkey were spent in a series of endless meetings... meetings that today I have no recollection of whatsoever. What I do remember is that at the end of the second day we were bundled into buses and taken for a photo opportunity with the then prime minister Ismet Inönü. As we lined up with Ismet *Paşa* (I was standing to his left), he spotted the five-year-old son of one of the Peace Corps staff whose father had brought him along for reasons known only to himself. The prime minister no sooner noticed the child than he stepped forward and motioned the little boy to approach. Pushed from behind by his father he advanced slowly. When he came within reach, Ismet *Paşa* leaned down (given his diminutive stature he didn't have all that far to lean) and, in the Turkish fashion, gently pinched both of the youngster's cheeks. The child's response was to begin shrieking. Inönü, clearly unnerved by this unexpected reaction, leaned forward once again and softly addressed the boy in perfect English: "Don't cry, please don't cry, little man." I am not sure that anyone else present, aside from the child and I, heard what he said. But his soothing words had the desired effect and the little boy stopped his hysterical outburst as abruptly as

Ismet Inönü meets the Turkey V Peace Corps volunteers

ıt had begun. We posed for our group photo, I shook the hand of one of the founders of the Turkish Republic, and we were off to yet another meeting.

It was a number of years later that I came to realize just what an historical event I had witnessed. Ismet Inönü, the man who had worn out his interlocutors at the Lausanne Peace Conference in 1923 by exaggerating his deafness and refusing to be rushed into anything (partly on the grounds that he did not understand the language they were speaking), had actually spoken English in my presence. I may be one of the few, or perhaps the only, living persons, who can state for certain that Ismet *Paşa* knew English... for I actually heard him speak it less than forty-eight hours after my arrival in Turkey.

PART II
THE BEREKETLI YEARS
(October 1964-February 1966)

Chapter 3

From Ankara to Balıkesir & beyond

After what seemed like an eternity, but in reality couldn't have been more than a week, we sat down to learn where we would be spending the next two years of our lives. I had hopes of finding myself in a coastal area – it didn't matter whether it was the Black Sea, Aegean or Mediterranean – but those fantasies were soon dashed when I was informed that I had been assigned to a village called Bereketli, that was in the northwestern Anatolian province of Balıkesir. Furthermore, accompanying me to Bereketli was a young female volunteer named Bonnie Landes, one of my cohorts whom I hadn't really gotten to know very well during the three months of our training. As the Peace Corps staff hadn't had the foresight to bring a map of Turkey to the meeting, I rushed down to the nearest bookstore (the old Tarhan's in Kızılay), to purchase a map of Turkey and find out just where it was that I was headed. I managed to locate Balıkesir on my new map but that is as far as I got. It seemed that the toponym 'Bereketli' had not yet found its way onto the available cartography.

Bright and early the next morning, we said our goodbyes to our fellow volunteers who were heading east, south and north, and those of us going west climbed into a minibus for the trip to what for me was still nowhere. I was somewhat heartened to find that my girlfriend Jeanne (who less than a year later was to become my first wife) was at least heading west as well. In her case it was to a village in Bilecik, that on my map seemed to be not all that far from Balıkesir. As we moved west from Polatlı to Eskişehir to Bilecik, Bursa and beyond, I remember thinking that I really had no idea what I was doing. For, despite the never-ending round of lectures, nobody had ever explained to my satisfaction just what being a Peace Corps volunteer entailed, and, in particular, what working in rural community development meant. It was little satisfaction to realize that my fellow sixty-eight companions had no more idea than I as to what they were supposed to spend the next two years doing. What we had been told was that we would be working with members of the Ministry of Education's newly created *Halk Eğitim Müdürlüğü* (Adult Education Directorate), the forerunner of what eventually was to become the Ministry of Village Affairs (*Köy İşleri Bakanlığı*). As events would soon prove, the representatives of this newly created body had as little idea as we did as to just what our role was supposed to be.

In retrospect it seems that when the Peace Corps entered Turkey in 1962, it knew as little about Turkey, as the United States was to know about Iraq when it entered that country forty years later. Planning in advance was not (and still is not) America's strong point.

After what seemed like a never-ending bus ride, broken only by the occasional stop to let off pairs of our compatriots, Bonnie and I found ourselves alone on the minibus that continued to move steadily westward. By this time night had fallen, and when we finally pulled into Balıkesir the city had already rolled up the sidewalks for the evening and we were unceremoniously dumped in front of the less-than-inspiring *Otel Özgür Palas* (Hotel Özgür Palace). There was no one to greet us, nor did the concierge seem to know that we were expected, but aided by my growing vocabulary (a week in Ankara had added at least ten words to my Turkish), I managed to get us a couple of rooms and figure out that the dining room was still open. In time, the *Otel Özgür Palas*'s restaurant was to become one of my favorite eating spots in Balıkesir, but my first impression of the hotel was less than impressive. It soon got worse as, having climbed two flights of stairs lugging all my worldly possessions, I entered my room only to find that it had five beds, two of which were already occupied by other men. In those days, even in the provincial capitals of Anatolia, one rented a bed, not a room, in a hotel.

The next morning, after a sleepless night due to the incessant snoring of one of my room-mates, the Balıkesir *Halk Egitim Müdürü* (Adult Education Director) arrived at the hotel and, with the help of a dictionary and a great deal of sign language, made it clear that he was going to accompany us out to the village of Bereketli. However, before we began the last leg of our journey, we were going to pay the mandatory visit to the governor of the province. When we arrived at the *Vilayet* (Government Office) and were ushered into the presence of the Governor (*Vali*), a man with whom, in time, I would have an up-and-down relationship, we were also introduced to a middle-aged woman who had been summoned to be our interpreter, in keeping with her position as the head of the English Language Department at the local high school. The governor began issuing what sounded like a series of rapid fire orders and after a couple of minutes of non-stop harangue paused for the interpreter to convey his words for our benefit. There was just one problem, while our translator probably knew far more English grammar than I did (or ever will), she couldn't really speak the language that she spent her life instructing others in. As it became increasingly clear that there was no communication, the Governor's level of irritation went up accordingly. He began to berate first the school teacher, and then, when I attempted to intervene, turned his wrath on me. Thus began what was to become one of the more rocky relationships I was to experience in the next two years. By the time we finally left his office it had become clear that: a) he thought we were spies; b) he expected weekly reports from me (delivered in person) on my activities in the village; and, c) I clearly had not managed to make a new friend. As fate would have it, I was to see a great deal of this gentleman in the next year, and some time was to pass before either of us would modify our first opinions with regard to the other.

Somewhat shaken, we climbed into a waiting jeep for the forty-five minute ride to our new home. As we slowly moved from the hustle and bustle of Balıkesir out into the countryside, I suddenly realized I was already beginning to miss the familiarity of the *Otel Özgür Palas*, if not my two unwelcome roommates of the previous evening. After what seemed like an endless ride we approached a turn in the dirt road we were on and saw a group of a couple of hundred men, women and children, waiting to welcome us to Bereketli. They scooped up our luggage, and I proceeded to shake a couple of hundred hands as we walked the last kilometer into the village, and I repeated the phrase *hoş bulduk* (the thank you one says in response to a welcoming greeting) over and over again.

Before reaching the village, in answer to the query *isminiz nedir?* (what is your name?), I had replied 'Heath' several dozen times, only to have my questioners repeat what I said back to me as 'Hit' (the 'th' sound being non-existent in Turkish), over and over again. It was as 'Hit' or, Hit *Bey* (Mr Heath), or Hit *Ağabey* (elder brother Heath) that I would be known for the next two years. In time, this version of my name was to be the cause of frequent misunderstanding, due to its proximity to the Turkish word "it" eaning a female dog or bitch. I soon learned that one of the more common forms of insulting someone in Bereketli was to refer to them as an *it oğlu it* (son of a bitch). On more than one occasion in the ensuing months, I was introduced by one or another village friend to strangers as "*bizim Amerikalı,* Hit *Bey,*" ('our American, Mr Heath'), only to find my friends lectured about the impropriety of referring to God's guest (*tanrı misafiri*) as an *it* (bitch). All this, however, was in the future. For the moment I was busy meeting my new neighbors, and trying to get used to responding to the name Hit.

It was a hot day and by the time we reached the village square in front of the coffee house I was both exhausted and in an advanced state of culture shock. The one thing I wasn't was hungry.

Chapter 4

Eating a sheep in the village *meydan*

I was ushered into the nearby coffee house and began to consume the first of what, by the end of the day, was to be at least two dozen small glasses of scalding hot tea sweetened with several spoonfuls of sugar. With each glass someone handed me a cigarette (I hadn't smoked much before that afternoon) that I accepted and lit as if instinctively knowing that they were sharing what little they had with me. It was only later that I realized that my first cigarettes had all been store bought, for Bereketli was a tobacco-growing village and in the normal course of events everyone rolled and smoked their own home-grown tobacco. However, in 1964 smoking tobacco that had not first been sold to the state and taxed was a crime punishable by, what for the villagers was, a stiff fine. Therefore, knowing that an official from the provincial capital was scheduled to accompany their new American guests, the *Muhtar* (elected village head) Kâmil Aslantekin, had insisted that everyone put aside their own tobacco pouches and smoke the store-bought variety. As this meant either the cheapest brand on the market *Üçüncü* (Third) or the second cheapest *Ikinci* (Second), I have a recollection of my throat burning due to the unaccustomed smoke, of dozens of faces pressed up close to mine, and a steady stream of conversation of which I may have comprehended only

The village *meydan*

ten percent. Seated next to me, round a wobbly small square table, were several individuals who, in the coming months, were to become close friends. Indeed one, the *Muhtar* himself, would prove to be the elder brother I had never had. For the moment they were strangers who, it seemed, were intent on talking me to death.

Noticeably missing from our gathering was Bonnie, my female compatriot, who had been quickly whisked off to an equally incomprehensible grueling by the distaff side of the Bereketli populace. My only real recollection of the next hour or so is of endless faces and voices. When the official from the capital who had accompanied us spoke, silence ensued and the villagers (probably in hopes of learning what I was doing there) respectfully listened to the representative of the state. To say that I was in shock would almost certainly be an understatement.

My sense of helplessness was heightened when, after half a dozen glasses of tea and an equal number of strong cigarettes, we were ushered into the square in front of the coffee house where a table and seven chairs had been brought from the school house. The *Muhtar* (Kâmil Aslantekin), the village school teacher (Mustafa *Hoca*), the Adult Education Director from Balıkesir, Bonnie (who had miraculously reappeared) and I were now joined by two young men (Kemal and Yusuf), whom, I was to learn later, were the Adult Education Department instructors in, respectively, a woodworking and a masonry course, that the teenage boys of the village were to be enrolled in the coming year. The seven of us sat down, with virtually the entire eight hundred residents of the village gathered round watching, and proceeded to eat (in some six courses) a rather large sheep. I quickly learned that this particular animal had parts I had never dreamed of consuming, including a head, complete with eye-balls! Before I was allowed to rise from that table in the square I had sampled them all. There was no longer any doubt in my mind whatsoever: I had undoubtedly made a serious mistake in coming to Turkey.

After this feast, that lasted well over two hours, the Adult Education Director stood up to take his leave and it suddenly dawned on me that my last link with the outside world was about to be broken. The departure of this official and his jeep meant that I really was staying on in Bereketli. I didn't dwell on this for too long, as in the course of the past hour I had become increasingly aware of an ever-growing need to find a toilet. The combination of the endless cups of tea (that had resumed as the meal neared its climax), the food I had eaten, and the fact that my last visit to the bathroom had been some ten hours earlier in the *Otel Özgür Palas* in Balıkesir, had culminated in a need to relieve myself that was rapidly approaching a critical stage. My discomfort must have been evident, because while I was desperately trying to come up with the correct manner of asking for a toilet in Turkish, the *Muhtar* motioned to me. I got up and accompanied him to the courtyard of the village *câmii* (mosque), and was introduced to the hole in the ground that was to serve my needs for the next year. I took the opportunity, having relieved my bladder, to empty my stomach as unobtrusively as possible (although some time later Kâmil *Bey* told me that he had heard me throwing up the meal I had been eating for the past two hours), as either the six courses of sheep, the eyeball, or the several slabs of sweetened *kabak* (cooked pumpkin) with which my initial foray into the cuisine of Bereketli ended, had resulted in a very upset stomach.

Having taken care of the essentials I began to feel that I might just live, and so we proceeded (still within the confines of the mosque compound) up a flight of stairs to my new home. It was a room that in the late 19th century had served as the classroom where village boys had been taught to memorize the *Qur'an* (Koran), a practice frowned upon in post-coup 1964 secular Turkey, and that prior to my arrival (and thereafter as well) was the *Muhtar Odası* (Mayor's Office), or *Köy Odası* (Village Room). I was pleased to see that next to the *yer yatak* (mattress rolled out on the floor) were the sum total of my belongings, that had been augmented before my arrival with a 'Peace Corps Library' (some 150 books in English – most of which I had read), and my own personal medical kit (filled with all manner of things designed to keep me alive until I could get to a doctor should the need arise), and a bag of assorted sports equipment. The books and sports equipment were untouched, but the medical kit had clearly been examined by numerous hands. It was only some time later that I was to learn that when these packages had arrived (a week before my humble self), my hosts, who were just as curious as I was about what I was supposed to be doing in their midst, had decided on the basis of the contents of my medical kit, that I was just what they had been praying for: a doctor.

I don't remember the rest of the day. I do know that by the time I was finally able to extract myself from the hands of my hosts, I felt like I had a slight fever. I opened my medical kit, took a couple of aspirins, paid a quick visit to the bathroom (that I shared with the rest of the village), and fell into a deep sleep in my new home. I know it was deep, because when the mice with whom I was to live for the next year began playing *cirit* (jereed) across my chest and face, I was so exhausted that all I did was brush them off and go back to sleep. Thus began what was to be two of the most pivotal and important years of my life.

Chapter 5

The longest invitation list in the world & meat every day

It was several months before I was to learn that while I had been becoming acquainted with my new four-legged bedtime companions on my first night in Bereketli, the men of the village had been summoned by the *Muhtar* to an unprecedented meeting in the largest of the village coffee houses. The topic of discussion was me and the question to be resolved was how the village was to feed this *tanrı misafiri* (unexpected overnight guest) who had suddenly appeared on their doorstep. While village custom dictated that any stranger was to be hosted for three days and nights, this one (me) was planning to stay for two years. The problem was that I was a male and unmarried, and therefore automatically assumed to be unable to take care of myself (no similar concern was expended on behalf of Bonnie, who, being a woman, was naturally thought to be capable of looking after her own needs). I was the problem and the meeting was called to determine how I was to be looked after and fed.

The heads of the one hundred and twenty-eight households of Bereketli had all answered the *Muhtar*'s summons, and, after a great deal of discussion, it was decided that on a rotating basis each family in

My room in the mosque courtyard

the village would host me for a twenty-four hour period. To organize this undertaking, a list was circulated and one by one each man of the village signed his name (or scrawled his mark as the case might be), thereby pledging to host me for a day. Forty-three years later, that list, albeit now somewhat tattered, is still one of the few possessions that has accompanied me step by step throughout my life. From time to time I take it out and read over the names of old friends and acquaintances (almost all of whom are now deceased) and recall what was the most spontaneous act of human kindness of which I have to this date been the recipient.

Before the meeting adjourned, some time was devoted to what my hosts should plan to serve me. Given the fact that every man in attendance had stood round earlier that day watching while I devoured a fair part of a large sheep, there was a consensus that their American liked meat and therefore it was decided that I should be fed meat at least once a day. The only person in attendance who could have disabused them of the view that I was a meat lover was the *Muhtar* who was far too clever to do so. There was also some discussion regarding where I was to be fed and again a consensus was reached that for breakfast a tray would be delivered to the *Muhtar Odası* on my behalf, while at noon I would join my host of the day at his coffee house (there were three in the village separated by politics and/or age) where food would be brought from his home. In the evening I would join my host, together with his family and friends (sometimes with Bonnie and usually with the *Muhtar* and village school teacher also in attendance) in his home.

What this meant was that by the time I had been in Bereketli for four months I would have been a guest in literally every home and met and come to know every man, woman and child in the village. That is exactly what happened. For the next one hundred and twenty-eight days I was fêted in home after home, and, night after night, the menu included some form of meat: a chicken, a goose, a piece of lamb, or *sucuk* (garlic-flavored sausage). In short, people (many of whom did not eat any meat from *bayram* to *bayram*, i.e., religious holiday to religious holiday), went out of their way to ensure that their *tanrı misafiri* never sat down to an evening meal without some form of meat being placed before him. The poorer families went so far as to borrow a chicken from their neighbors, but Hit *Bey* always ate meat. This sense of *misafirperverlik* (hospitality) is the overwhelming impression I have of my life in Bereketli, even prior to the time (some six months later) that I learned about the meeting held on my first night, and long before I had come to realize that everyone didn't eat meat every day in Bereketli.

Chapter 6

I still hear the cries of *'ye, ye'* ('eat, eat') in the occasional nightmare

Within a few short days of my arrival in Bereketli, life had begun to enter a routine. There would be a knock on the door of my room at 5 a.m., accompanied by a tray bearing bread, olives, cheese, jam and tea, usually delivered by my host for the day or by one of his children. Once every two or three days this routine would vary and instead of being greeted by the expected tray I would find my host empty-handed. This was a sign that we would be going to his coffee house to have our breakfast there together.

The coffee houses in Bereketli were three in number. The largest, that was located in the village square, was the *köy kahvesi* (official village coffee house), that, in my day, had been leased to Bereketli's sole Korean War veteran, Şakir. As it was owned by the village it was open to all, but clearly under the purview of the *Muhtar* Kâmil, who, like all village head men in post-coup 1964 Turkey, had been selected for his post due to his being a member of the Republican People's Party. While personally extremely popular (a fact borne out a year later when he was elected with 80% of the vote to the position that he had initially been appointed to), his politics however were not embraced by the majority of the electorate who were firmly committed to the

The weekly baking day

Democrat Party of the late Adnan Menderes. The Democrats had their own coffee house as well (it was owned and operated by Arif Aslantekin, an uncle of the *Muhtar*), and on those days when my host happened to be a partisan of that party, it would be my first stop of the day. In addition, the *delikanlıs* (literally, 'wild bloods.' i.e., young unmarried males) had their own establishment and, as by age and status, I too was one of them, I likewise always spent a part of every day in their midst. In short, I spent a lot of time drinking tea, smoking cigarettes and listening to the news on *Radyo Ankara*.

One thing was certain: from the moment I left my room in the morning until I closed the door at night I was never alone in Bereketli. I quickly learned that part of being a good host (and the entire village were my hosts) meant never leaving your guest alone. In an Anatolian village, spending time alone is definitely considered an abnormality. The only people who do so are the shepherds, who are regarded with suspicion for having spent so much time alone. After all, everyone knows that the solitude associated with tending one's flocks has given the world monotheism and the prophets Moses, Jesus and Mohammad.

My most frequent companion was the *Muhtar* Kâmil. He was, after all, responsible for my well-being, and in the same manner that he had arranged for my feeding and lodging, he became my first (and closest) friend in my new life. He was one of those rare individuals, who, without the benefit of much formal education (he had two years beyond the primary school level), were truly wise in all the things that count in life. It is to him that I really owe my lifelong fascination with, and love of, Turkey and its people. If he was otherwise occupied he made certain that one of his associates (members of his *ihtiyar heyeti,* or council of elders) was delegated to accompany me.

As evening approached, I would be summoned by that day's host for dinner and, accompanied usually by the *Muhtar*, and sometimes by Bonnie as well, would visit a new home each day. As my first Fall in Bereketli was a particularly wet one, and the village streets (or what passed for such) were always muddy, I had taken to wearing a pair of high lace-up boots that were particularly inappropriate for entering and leaving village homes. They meant that before entering each new house I had to stop, unlace my boots, take them off, and then repeat the process in reverse upon leaving. As most days I was in and out of half a dozen houses, this process quickly became a major nuisance. Unlike me, many of the older men of Bereketli wore a much more practical kind of footwear known as *mest lastik*, a sock-like zippered soft leather shoe (*mest*) over which a pair of short rubber goulashes (*lastik*) were pulled. Upon entering a house all the wearer of this footwear had to do was slip off the outer rubber goulashes. Designed for facilitating the required five times daily ablutions and prayers, it quickly became apparent to me that they were the only practical solution for life on the muddy streets and paths of Bereketli. In turn, I promised myself that on my next visit to Balıkesir my very first purchase would be a pair of *mest lastik*.

In the meantime I continued to go through the annoying ritual of lacing and unlacing my impractical boots. When I finally got them off and entered the house there would be a *yer sofrası* (a round wooden tray on short legs) in the middle of the floor, and we would immediately take our places round it (together with the host and maybe one or two or his relatives or neighbors), and the women of the house would begin bringing in the evening meal. The food was simple and generally very good. Word quickly got out that I was particularly fond of the village staple known as *kuru fasulye* (dried beans), and, from that point on, most meals included a common dish of beans into which we dipped our spoons. It and every course was accompanied by large slabs of bread that the host would cut from giant round loafs. I quickly learned that each family baked but once a week, and it made a significant difference as to whether I was their guest on or near baking day, or several days later. For when it was fresh the bread (made of mixed grains) was edible, but when, after a few days, it grew stale, it became hard and (for me) barely digestible. Running the gamut of two to five dishes, each meal was accompanied by plenty of *ayran* and yogurt. Word also quickly spread that Hit *Bey* liked onions and each evening there would be a whole onion and a knife next to my seat. I ate whatever was set before me, for there was no way that I was ever going to suggest to my generous hosts that I didn't appreciate their hospitality. Yet no matter how much I ate, night after night, in house after house, the refrain from the men and womenfolk alike was always the same: "*Ye, ye, hiç bir şey yemiyorsun*" (Eat, eat, you aren't eating anything). Initially, I assumed this was just exaggerated politeness on their part but as I heard this refrain night after night (and sometimes at noon in the coffee houses as well), it began to get to me. I began to pay close attention to just how many times I (and the other guests) dipped our spoons into the common bowl. It was clear that I was eating more than my share and yet in each house all I heard was "*ye, ye.*" I'd like to claim that I figured out what the problem was in a matter of days, but in reality it was closer to a month before I began to comprehend. No one paid any attention to how many times you partook of the common dish, that would have been impolite. What determined whether or not you were eating enough was simply the amount of bread you ate. The etiquette of Bereketli demanded that you eat at least two large slices at each meal, only when you had done so could your host be assured that you were full. For bread was the staff of life, the rest was just the extra. My mistake had been not to pay close-enough attention to my fellow guests. Once I realized what the problem was, I began dutifully eating the required kilogram of bread and the refrain quickly changed to "*Maşallah, yemeğimizi seviyorsun*" (Praise to God, now you like our food).

Try as hard as I could there was one aspect of the local cuisine that I never managed to develop a taste for. Given that I had arrived in the village in the early Fall, fresh fruit was not in season, and for my first four months virtually every meal ended with large thick slabs of *kabak tatlısı* (cooked pumpkin) doused in *pekmez* (grape syrup). Here too, I quickly learned that etiquette demanded you consume at least two large slabs of pumpkin and, while night after night I managed to do so, I have never eaten *kabak tatlısı* since leaving Bereketli.

Chapter 7

Who's that playing with my butt?

There was one lesson that the instructors in the training phase of my preparation as a Peace Corps volunteer had drummed thoroughly into my head. Over and over they had warned us about what they thought were the sexual mores of Turkish village life, and endlessly reiterated the necessity of never showing any attention whatsoever to the young girls or women of the villages we were going to be living in. Failure to follow this advice, they warned, would have dire consequences, and so much as a smile could lead to expulsion from the village, or, barring that, finding oneself leveraged into an unwanted marriage. I took these warnings to heart, and despite the fact that almost from my first day in Bereketli I was greeted by every girl and woman as I moved about the village, I was particularly careful never to return anything more than a simple *merhaba* (hello).

These admonitions also stressed the fact that as unmarried foreigners, Bonnie and I should likewise be sure that we were never alone together. In retrospect I realize that I likewise had absorbed this advice, and with the typical insensitiveness of youth, was so careful to observe both the letter and the spirit of this injunction that I provided little in the way of support for my fellow volunteer, whose role as a single woman adjusting to life in a Turkish village was to be far more difficult than mine. For in addition to having to deal with all the aspects related to survival, that I as a man was sheltered from due to the belief of our hosts that I was incapable of looking after myself, Bonnie also had to contend with the village women, most of whom had not even enjoyed the benefit of a primary school education and therefore spoke a version of Turkish that even a year later I was still to have trouble understanding.

In short, as concerns both the distaff side of the village and my fellow volunteer, I was intent on showing not the slightest sign of interest. This, the only part of our training that seemed to have stuck with me, meant that I was determined to live like a village man among village men, without being seemingly aware of the fact that they too had lives beyond the coffee shop.

This was fine until one evening, while the guest in a home at the far end of the village, I felt a foot clearly pressing against my backside. That evening, as on most nights, after the dishes had been cleared from the *sofra*, the womenfolk of the house and some of their neighbors entered the room and sat in a circle on the floor behind us to listen to the post-dinner conversation. As was often the case the room was small and there wasn't all that much space between the inner circle of men and the outer circle of women. My initial reaction was to scoot forward, but there really wasn't any place to go, and for the next hour I continued to receive the same incessant unwanted massage on my posterior. When finally the *Muhtar* rose, signaling that it was time to go, I ventured a quick glance behind me and saw that the party responsible for the unsolicited attention was an attractive young girl of sixteen or seventeen. Sensing my glance she smiled coyly and I walked out of the house feeling that I was headed for (if not already in) serious trouble.

As fate would have it, less than a week later I was invited to the house next door to the one in which I had first encountered the young girl and, once again, after dinner we were joined by our hostess and her neighbors. Almost immediately, I felt the same small foot gently rubbing my backside. By this time I had begun to impress my fellow villagers with my ability at remembering names (indeed, after those

The fair Ayşe at the fountain

first four months I knew virtually everyone in Bereketli by name), and one of the daily post-dinner rituals was being introduced to everyone in the house. It was in this manner that I learned that the young girl who seemed to have a fascination with my backside was named Ayşe and she was the daughter of one of the village elders named Mehmet.

I could hardly wait for the evening to come to an end, and, on the walk back to my room next to the mosque, I seriously considered broaching the subject with my friend the *Muhtar,* but hesitated given his closeness to the girl's father who was, after all, a member of his Council of Elders.

I now began to dread what had been the highlight of my days, namely, the approach of evening signaling that soon I would be summoned to dinner. When breakfast was brought to me in the morning I began enquiring about each day's host, about where in the village they lived, and on those days when it was clear that their homes were nowhere near that of Ayşe's, I breathed a sigh of relief. Then one night, in a house at the opposite end of the village from my caressing little friend, I once again felt a familiar foot stroking itself against my backside. I had forgotten that young Ayşe might have relatives who lived in other parts of the village.

When my four-month stint as a guest in each house ended I breathed another sigh of relief knowing that aside from what seemed to be quite frequent encounters with Ayşe on the street, where on each occasion I was greeted by a coy smile and friendly words, to that I responded with my standard *merhaba,* I was unlikely to find myself subjected to that insistent foot.

It was several months later, while sitting in the coffee house, that I announced to the assembled men that I was going to get married and would be leaving the following week to do so. After the expected round of questions as to why I wasn't going to marry Bonnie (her parents had paid a visit the previous month to Bereketli and the general consensus was that this meant that they must have plenty of money, a fact that made Bonnie a particularly desirous candidate for matrimony), and why I wasn't going to have the wedding in Bereketli, one of my companions, a loveable giant known as *Hırsız* Ibrahim (due to his propensity for picking up lighters and pens left on the coffee house tables), spoke up and said "Hit, this is the best news we've ever heard." Given his well-known sense of wit I was anticipating a punchline, but nonetheless responded as expected with "What do you mean?" His answer more than shocked me. He said, "We were all beginning to wonder about you. You don't have anything to do with boys and we knew you obviously didn't like girls." "Stop right there," I said "What do you mean I don't like girls?" "Well" he continued, "Mehmet's daughter Ayşe has been throwing it in your face ever since you arrived and you never showed the slightest interest." It was out. The secret I had been living with for months wasn't a secret at all. It was known to everyone in the village, and my failure to respond to those little feet had led to a great deal of coffee house speculation about my sexual proclivities. This was a lesson I did not forget: there are no secrets in a Turkish village. Everything is known to every one.

I've sometimes wondered how the course of my life might have changed had I shown the slightest response to Ayşe's gentle flirting. I might even still be sipping glasses of sweet tea in Bereketli.

Chapter 8

My foray into fasting, or my first *Ramazan*

I had only been in Bereketli for a couple of months when *Ramazan* (the month when Muslims fast from sun up to sun down) arrived. Realizing that it would be unfair to expect my generous hosts to cook for and feed me when they themselves were fasting, I decided that the best course of action was for me to fast as well. Aware of the fact that every move I made was known and indeed discussed at length, I took my decision seriously and really fasted. There were a couple of downsides to this decision. First, it meant that my normal 5 a.m. wake-up call came even earlier. Second, it meant that I was expected to eat a full meal before sunrise, that is, at 4 a.m., before I had even had the chance to wash my face and clear my head.

The problem of getting up earlier was that I simply wasn't getting enough sleep as it was. It wasn't that the residents of Bereketli went to bed too late. Far from it, by *yatsı* (the evening prayer at two hours after sunset) the village had pretty well rolled up its non-existent sidewalks, and aside from the occasional flicker of oil lamps or candles, was shrouded in complete darkness. No, the problem was me. I had purchased a battery-run radio and one night had discovered that at 11 p.m. on the "Voice of America" there was a great hour of jazz. Not

My alarm clock, the local mosque, from the window of my house

only did jazz happen to be my favorite music, but with the knowledge that if I stayed awake till 11 p.m. I would be transformed from Bereketli to New Orleans and beyond, it quickly became an essential part of my daily ritual.

The only problem was that when I was woken up for breakfast at 5 a.m., I really had not enjoyed the requisite amount of sleep. A nap in the afternoon was out of the question, as whenever I tried it my door opened repeatedly with friends enquiring as to whether I was ill. The result was continual sleep deprivation. Now, the arrival of *Ramazan* meant that I was getting even less rest, as *sahur* (the morning meal before the sun rose and the fast began) made its appearance at 4 a.m. However, unwilling to break my jazz-hour routine, and equally unwilling to eat a huge meal in what was for me the middle of the night, I went through the month of *Ramazan* hungry, sleepy and more than a little irritable. I did, however, keep to the fast not even sneaking the occasional cigarette or glass of water. This behavior, as everything else I did in Bereketli, was noted by one and all and ultimately led to some interesting encounters.

Having seen that their American, while an unbeliever, was fasting, my new friends decided that I must be well disposed towards accepting the true faith, and began planning my conversion. However, having little or no confidence in the local *Hoca* (a product of the village as were they), and realizing that I had a lot of books and therefore must know how to read, they decided to enlist the aid of the *Imam* of Balıkesir's Friday Mosque, the *Zaganos Paşa Câmii*. Not far into *Ramazan*, I was informed that I was to have a special guest the next day and, as announced, the leading religious authority from the provincial capital arrived in Bereketli to begin my introduction to the true faith. Forewarned as to my proclivity for reading he brought with him a Turkish-Arabic *Qur'an* and several books designed to instruct me in the practices of Islam. Having listened patiently for several hours, I finally managed to extricate myself from his grasp and, after having promised to faithfully read all the literature, bid my guest goodbye.

At one point in the conversation he had broached the rather painful question of circumcision and seemed genuinely pleased to learn that I had suffered that indignity as a baby and that my heretofore reticence to embrace Islam was not due to a fear of the knife. This was but the first of several encounters with this gentleman and while he never did convince me to convert we did enjoy many an hour of discussion, sweetened by countless glasses of tea.

The worst part of *Ramazan* was the waiting. As that year it came at a time when the work in the fields was done, and before the first snow, so that most of the men in the village simply sat around all day in the coffee houses (without the boredom-relieving diversion of cards, backgammon or dominoes – all such enjoyment being frowned upon during *Ramazan*), periodically asking the *kahveci* (café owner) what time it was. By an hour before sunset, the unfortunate *kahveci* had been told at least a dozen times that he was late in lighting the fire to heat the water for the long-awaited first cup of tea. At about the same time, tins and pouches of tobacco began to appear on the tables, and shortly thereafter the first cigarettes began to be rolled. The real purists in our midst refrained from actually licking the paper and, instead, simply laid out small pieces of newspaper (cigarette papers being prohibitively expensive) with a measured amount of tobacco in each, waiting for the *Hoca* to climb the minaret and announce that the day's fast had ended. A few minutes later one of the young boys was ordered to stand outside on the steps to let us know the moment he saw the *Hoca* begin walking toward the minaret. After that there were calls to the *kahveci* to begin pouring the first round of tea. By the time the call to prayer began to echo from the minaret, the assembled body was all in a fever of anticipation. For the next fifteen minutes we sipped our tea and smoked. Only when the important rituals were completed did anyone get up from the table and head for their home in search of sustenance more filling than caffeine and nicotine.

Shortly after the end of *Ramazan*, my cynical friend *Hırsız* Ibrahim and I were sitting in the coffee house rolling our home-made cigarettes with a group of men, when he turned to me and asked "Hit, do you remember *Ramazan?*" To which I replied, "Of course, why do you ask?" He continued "Did you really fast? Are you sure you never

snuck a glass of water or a cigarette?" I replied that I had indeed fasted. He laughed, and said "Then you are the only person in the whole
village that did. Even the Hoca sneaks the occasional cigarette." I
never really knew if this exchange worked to my benefit, or whether it
just made me seem even odder.

Chapter 9

Keeping warm on purloined wood in a Bereketli winter

Winter came early and cold to western Anatolia in 1964. Bereketli was just far enough up in the foothills to bear the brunt of it. I had purchased a small tin *soba* (stove), and together with my new *mest lastik* (that indeed I had acquired on one of my first forays to the city), I naively thought that I was prepared for whatever the weather brought. I wasn't sure just what I was supposed to burn in my stove, for while most of my neighbors had clearly been stockpiling *tezek* (dried cow dung), I possessed neither cattle nor water buffalos, the two essential producers of that particular kind of fuel. As I did on average ten times a day, I questioned the *Muhtar* on the matter, and was relieved when he replied that he had already taken care of it and that there would soon be a load of wood delivered to my lodging. What he didn't tell me was that the woodsmen upon whom I was dependent were *tahtacıs* (Alevis who lived on *Kaz Dağ*), who made their living illegally cutting and selling wood from the government forests. He did tell me that he had ordered two loads of wood for me and that each would cost 10 TL ($1 at the then rate of exchange). He suggested that I keep this sum available as one never really knew when the delivery might occur.

My tin *soba* and bed

A couple of nights later I was awakened at 2 a.m. by a loud bang-
ing on my door. I did not have to worry about getting dressed as it
was already so cold that I had taken to sleeping in layers of clothing,
so I simply fumbled round for my flashlight and went down to see
what was happening. I opened the door to find myself facing two
rather large dark men with drooping mustaches and two very large
camels each bearing a huge load of wood. It seems the *Muhtar* had
also neglected to tell me that the woodcutters delivered in the middle
of the night (a necessary precaution against the possibility of arrest by
the gendarmes who did not look kindly upon their form of livelihood),
nor that their delivery vehicle of choice was the camel. Recovering
from my initial shock, I showed them where the wood should go and
went back upstairs to get the necessary 20 TL. By the time I had
returned the camels had knelt down, the straps securing their loads
had been loosened, and my two guests were quickly and silently trans-

Bereketli's wood delivery system

ferring my wood into the storage area beneath my room. The whole process took less than ten minutes, the money exchanged hands, and just as quickly as they had appeared they disappeared soundlessly into the night. Now I was truly set for the winter.

Before that long winter ended I was to have several more visits from my *tahtacı* friends, as even keeping my little *soba* burning all night long did little to temper the bone-chilling cold of my first Bereketli winter.

Chapter 10

Kekik yağı & the death of innocence

Less than a week after the arrival of my wood, I was once again awakened in the middle of the night by a hammering on my door. This time when I responded to the summons I was greeted not by camels, but by a young boy covered in snow (winter had chosen to officially arrive that night). I recognized him as the son of Mehmet Sadık Özkan, the head of a particularly poor family whose guest I had been a few days earlier. He was visibly shaken and speaking so quickly that all I understood was that someone was ill and he wanted me to accompany him. As I put on my coat and started to leave he grabbed my arm and motioned toward my medical kit that was sitting on the floor. I nodded, he picked it up, and we set off through blinding snow flurries towards the other end of the village. That was the beginning of what was to become the longest night of my life.

As we approached the house I saw a dim light through the windows and began to hear keening wails and piercing screams echoing into the darkness. Upon entering the door the din increased and I suddenly found myself in the midst of close to fifty women, who, without tempering their high-pitched wailing, parted and I moved forward into the middle of a small room. Before me on the floor was a beauti-

Winter arrives and turns mud into beauty

ful young girl lying rigidly with white froth bubbling from her mouth. By this time my initial vocabulary of two hundred words had grown two-fold, but instinctively I knew that it wasn't going to be adequate to deal with what I was facing. My medical kit appeared at my side, and accompanied by the never-ending wailing, I felt for a pulse and took the young girl's temperature. Having done so, I had completely exhausted my *doktorluk* (medical expertise). Knowing only that she was still alive and with no idea of what to do next, I looked up and saw the familiar face of my friend, the *Muhtar* Kâmil. I motioned him aside and in my best Turkish told him I had no idea what was wrong, but I was fairly certain if something wasn't done quickly, and that meant getting her to a hospital, the young girl, whose name I learned was Emine, was going to die. Someone had overheard our conversation and its contents quickly spread throughout the room. The impact of my diagnosis was felt immediately, and what had been an awful wailing grew in volume until I felt that my head was about to burst. The room, with what by now had grown to seventy-five occupants, was stifling and the din seemed only to grow in volume and intensity. An old woman was screaming at me (I later learned that she was what prior to my arrival had passed for the medical expert in the village), and I didn't understand a word she was saying. At some point, I began shouting for everyone to shut up and get out of the room. I can still hear my own voice at such a pitch that it had, at least temporarily, the effect of drowning out the cacophony of sounds surrounding me.

In response to my outburst some of the women left the room and those who remained reduced the volume of their wailing to a level that was almost bearable. The *Muhtar* and I went outside with a young man (whom later I learned was Emine's husband Ercan) and his father, and I repeated that there was only one course of action possible and that was to find someway to get Emine to the hospital in Balıkesir.

There were a few problems with my suggestion: firstly, what half an hour earlier had been snow flurries had turned into a real snow storm, and secondly, we were twenty-five kilometers from the nearest hospital. Finally, on top of all this, that night there was only one operative motor vehicle in the village that was a tractor with an open *römork* (trailer). Outside, where we were standing, the volume of the wailing had been reduced to vague crying noises emanating from the house and had been replaced by a blistering wind that whipped up the snow in painful flurries. Even standing next to the wall, the snow felt like tiny pieces of glass cutting into my exposed cheeks. My two week's growth of beard (I had immediately adopted the local fashion of shaving only every other week), was quickly turning into an icicle and we still had come to no decision.

For well over an hour I continued imploring the girl's husband to tell me what she had eaten, or if she had taken any medicine. He, as had the women in the house earlier, continued to insist that she had been perfectly well all day and had only eaten what the rest of the family had for dinner. I was fairly certain that we were facing some kind of poisoning, but there was no confirmation forthcoming from the family. Finally, in absolute desperation, I managed to explain that there was only one thing that might save her life and this entailed pumping her stomach – something that could only be done in a hospital. I still have no recollection of what words I used to get this message across, but, aided by the *Muhtar*, who, as was usually the case, sided with my diagnosis, we finally managed to get a grudging agreement from the family members and preparations began for our trip to Balıkesir.

A half hour later the tractor and its open trailer arrived, and six of us men carried the comatose girl on her *yer yatak* out of the house and laid her gently in its bed. As we did so, I remember thinking that this must be similar to how corpses were transported. That thought did little to settle my growing panic.

Two large sheets of heavy plastic were finally procured and having wrapped one firmly round the patient and tucked its edges under the mattress, six of us men climbed into the trailer with the second sheet of plastic held over our heads. It wasn't really large enough to do the job and while it kept most of the snow and some of the wind away from our patient, it did little to protect those who were holding it. I do know that it took us well over an hour to cover the first fifteen kilometers of our journey, guided by the tractor's sole headlight, that, rather than pointing at the snow-covered dirt track, veered eerily off into the sky, and by the time we had arrived at the half-way point, the village of Pamukçu, the side of my face that had been exposed to the snow was literally a solid sheet of ice. In Pamukçu there was a jeep that functioned as a taxi, and while one of my companions went to awaken its driver, I bent down, for what must have been the fiftieth time, to check and see if Emine was still with us. I felt a faint pulse, and, bolstered by that feeble sign of life, began urging my companions to continue on and not to wait for the jeep and its driver. Just as we were about to resume our trek the taxi arrived and after carefully lifting Emine onto the back seat, her husband, the *Muhtar* and I climbed aboard and we set off for the last leg of our journey to the capital. In my broken Tarzan-Turkish I insistently reiterated the same message to the distraught husband: if he didn't tell me what had actually happened there was simply no way the doctors were going to be able to help. Finally, after much urging he said "The baby was sick" (this was the first I had heard of a child's involvement – in reality, Emine had given birth just a week earlier) "and wouldn't nurse, so Emine found a bottle of medicine on the shelf and took two tablespoons of it." I enquired as to just what the medicine was, but the answer I received *"kekik yağı"* (oil of thyme) did not register in my vocabulary, so all the way to Balıkesir I kept repeating *kekik yağı, kekik yağı*, over and over again, in the hope of having something to tell the doctors upon our arrival. As it had taken me close to four hours to extract those two words, I wanted to make sure that the doctors didn't have to spend the same amount of time in making their diagnosis. I later was to learn that the reticence to share with me the fact that Emine had self-medicated was the typical fear of the villagers that they might be accused of some wrong-doing once they left the familiar womb of home and family and entered the city with its police and courts.

After what seemed like an eternity, our jeep pulled up in front of the hospital, and I went running in screaming for a doctor. The last time I had felt for a pulse it seemed even weaker than before, and I knew we didn't have much time. Suddenly, a young man in a white coat arrived and in perfect English asked what the matter was. Later, after Dr Özcan Hangül and I had become friends, he admitted that he had been frightened when he saw what appeared to be a crazed foreigner, covered in snow and ice, screaming in the corridor of his hospital. He gave no sign of this at the time however, and as quickly as possible I summarized the events of the past four hours, making sure to repeat the two words whose meaning I still did not know, *kekik yağı*, over and over again. A stretcher appeared and Emine was rushed into a nearby operating room. The doors closed and after what seemed like an eternity, but was in reality less than fifteen minutes, Özcan *Bey* appeared with the news that Emine had died.

To say that my life flashed before my eyes the moment I heard those words is hardly an exaggeration. I saw myself being shipped out of Turkey in disgrace blamed for the death of a young mother. Sometimes in moments of stress we humans tend to think of ourselves rather than those around us. Emine's husband Ercan, had just lost his wife of less than a year, the mother of his week-old infant son, and I was worried about what implications her death might have for me.

Perhaps something of my stress had communicated itself to Özcan *Bey*, because when I quit feeling sorry for myself, I heard him telling the *Muhtar* and Ercan that they owed me a debt of thanks, for my insistence on getting Emine to the hospital was in fact the only chance there had been of saving her life. Then he began berating them for not following my advice when it was first given, and repeated over and over again that had we managed to get her to the hospital even an hour earlier they would have been able to save her life. I will never forget that night as long as I live, nor will I forget the cold and snow, for it was just a foretaste of what was in store for the residents of Bereketli in the Winter of 1964.

Over several glasses of tea, Özcan *Bey* explained to me that *kekik yağı* was oil of thyme, a drop or two of which was a powerful heart stimulant, two tablespoons of which was a virtual death sentence. I later was to learn that the bottle in question had been purchased fifteen years earlier by a long-deceased relative. All little Emine knew was that her baby was sick, that medicine cured sickness, and this was the only medicine in the house. In the hope that the medicine she took would be passed via her milk to her ailing infant she had taken a fatal dose of oil of thyme. Özcan *Bey* refused to accept payment, and, after carefully placing the now cold corpse of Emine back into the jeep, we set off for the return trip to Bereketli.

Later, when I had gotten to know Özcan, his American wife Rose (whom he had met while undergoing his medical training in the United States) and their baby son Osman, better, I prevailed upon the good doctor to come to Bereketli one Sunday a month to run a free medical clinic for the villagers. His generous willingness to do so gave many of the residents of Bereketli their first glimpse of a real doctor. This didn't help me all that much however, because the *Muhtar* and the grieving husband accurately reported their conversation with the *Doktor Bey* (Hit *Bey*'s friend), and my unwarranted reputation as a 'healer,' far from what I had anticipated, grew and grew. It wasn't long before patients from surrounding villages began showing up on the doorstep of the American doctor. My advice to one and all never varied: you must get to Balıkesir and see Dr Özcan *Bey*. When it was clear they didn't have the means to get to the city, I often provided the bus fare. As the word was out that when Hit *Bey* says you need to see the doctor, you did so, I may have indirectly helped some people.

My friendship with Özcan *Bey* was put to the test, when after a few months of providing free medical services to the villagers of Bereketli, I invited him to bring his wife Rose and the baby Osman out to the village for a dinner in his honor. It was early summer, the weather was lovely, and the food was delicious. There was only one small drawback, tender city-bred baby Osman was virtually eaten alive by the fleas of Bereketli. When this occurred I realized that I really had adjusted to village life, for the fleas no longer seemed to find me worth biting. From then on when I saw the Hangüls it was in their home in Balıkesir.

Chapter 11

The villager (me) spends time in the provincial capital

One of the least pleasant aspects of my new life was a mandatory visit to the *Vali* (Governor) every Saturday morning (in those years government offices were still open six days a week). Shortly after my arrival the Governor had sent word to the *Muhtar* that he and I were to be in his office at precisely 10 a.m. each Saturday morning to provide him with a detailed update of my activities during the preceding week. Complying with this dictate was not at all an easy task.

The difficulty stemmed from several factors: on Saturdays neither of the two vintage buses that serviced the village ran, and there was only one truck from the *Nahiye* of Konakpınar (the county seat located five kilometers above us in the hills), that passed through Bereketli en route to Balıkesir and that happened to do so at the ungodly hour of 4:30 a.m. To catch a ride to the capital entailed getting up at 4 a.m., and after having removed the layers of clothing I wore at night, in a fruitless effort to protect myself from the cold, quickly getting dressed into something appropriate for the Governor, then running out to the road that passed near the village in order to flag down the passing truck. The only positive aspect of this part of the process was that, as the American guest of the *Nahiye,* whoever was riding in the cab was relegated into the back of the truck, and the *Muhtar* and I had the comfort of riding inside where we were protected from the elements, even if the heater in this particular vehicle never seemed to work.

On good days the ride to the capital took just over an hour, meaning that upon our arrival there were still four-and-a-half hours to kill before the scheduled appointment. There was not a great deal to do in Balıkesir at that time in the morning, and Saturday after Saturday I was taken to the only establishment that seemed to be open, the local *işkembeci,* where I was subjected to a bowl of garlic-enriched soup and a loaf of bread. I recognized the soup as that which I had eaten on my first night in Ankara (after the abortive visit to the brothels), but I still had no real idea what it was I was eating. The problem was that the only dictionary I had was a small pocket 'Langenscheidt,' that did not include any variant of the word *işkembe.* There being no visible option, week after week, I dutifully ate my loaf of bread and somehow managed to get what for me was an unpleasant tasting concoction down my throat. I wasn't yet familiar with the folk belief that a hot bowl of *işkembe çorbası* was considered by many to be the perfect ending for a night of heavy drinking and the only preventative for a hangover, but I was aware that at 5:30 a.m. the *Muhtar* and I were usually the only two sober patrons at the *Lezzet Işkembecisi* (Delicious Tripe Soup Restaurant).

It was a couple of months later, when my group of volunteers were summoned to Ankara for three days of meetings, that I was finally to learn just what it was that I had been eating. No sooner had I disembarked at Ankara train station than I jumped into a taxi and told the driver to take me to the *Tarhan Kitabevi* (bookstore) in Kızılay, where I asked him to wait for a couple of minutes. I ran into the store, found the Fahir Iz & H.C. Hony 'Turkish-English Dictionary,' located the word *işkembe* and realized that I had been eating 'tripe' infused with garlic every Saturday morning for the past several months. I have never done so again in the last forty-three years, a fact that I am all too well aware disqualifies me from even being considered as an 'Honorary Turk.' I tell myself that since I like virtually everything else in Turkey,

I deserve the right to at least say no to intestines cooked in garlic, or more accurately intestine soup over which garlic is poured.

After that brief interlude we returned to Balıkesir, where, after downing my less-than-appetizing breakfast, we still had close to four hours to kill prior to our command appearance before the Governor. After the first couple of trips I managed to convince Kâmil *Bey* that I was capable of finding my way round the city alone, and, as he always had things to do and people to see, we would go our separate ways after arranging to meet at the *Vilayet* (provincial capital) at precisely 9:50 a.m.

Almost simultaneously with my arrival in Bereketli I had come to realize that the one aspect of my former life that I was truly going to miss was a daily hot shower. Not only did my room not have hot water it had no water at all. This meant that when I wanted water, it had to be carried from the nearest fountain that was fortunately only a few meters from my door. One of the advantages of living in a mosque courtyard is the proximity to water that has to be available for the believers' ritual ablutions. That said, the rite of making several trips back and forth to the fountain with my earthenware pitcher, and then waiting for water to heat on top of my *soba*, was not an appealing prospect, and given the dust and/or mud that covered Bereketli throughout the year, I always seemed to feel slightly in need of a bath. This feeling grew progressively until the Saturday morning I happened to notice a Balıkesir establishment called the *Şehir Sıhhi Banyoları*, or the 'City Hygenic Public Bathhouse.' I wandered in and found myself in a steam-filled environment, complete with individual rooms containing bathtubs and showers, a seemingly never-ending flow of steaming hot water, and gigantic bath towels. From that moment on, my weekly *işkembe* breakfast was followed by a luxurious hour-long shower.

My next stop was the corner barber shop, where I would lose the previous week's growth of beard, followed by a refreshing facial massage. Then, doused in a variety of colognes, I would step out on the streets of Balıkesir, virtually a new man.

There was still one small problem. Even though my body was now sparkling, my outer clothes did not share my new found cleanliness. In time, I also managed to resolve this dilemma. Just round the corner from my bathhouse I discovered a small family-run hotel with ten rooms, one of which, while hardly bigger than a closet, was billed as a single. It couldn't have been anything else as it was only large enough to accommodate a small bed and an even smaller chair. The price was 3 TL (roughly thirty-five cents) per night, and I quickly negotiated a monthly rate of 50 TL. I now had a second home in Balıkesir, and the next weekend I brought my 'fit for the Governor' wardrobe with me and neatly hung it on the nails in my hotel room's walls. From that point on my Saturday morning ritual consisted of: the compulsory bowl of *işkembe*, followed by a hot bath, a shave, a change of clothing, and an hour of relaxation on my tiny bed, before the mandatory visit to the Governor's office. In time, as my relationship with my hotelier hosts blossomed, we worked out an arrangement whereby, when necessary, they could rent out my room in my absence (after promising to change the sheets should they do so), in return for which the mother of the family did my weekly wash.

Refreshed and clean, I would then set out for the *Vilayet* and waiting *Muhtar*. En route to my rendezvous with the provincial symbol of state authority, I would stop at the corner *büfe* and sample the newest soft drink entry into the Turkish market: a bottle of Coca Cola, or *Joja Jola*, as it was called locally. I did this, even on the coldest days, not because I particularly liked this beverage, but rather because it was something that once again served to remind me that there was still a world beyond that which I now found myself in. Thus fortified, I would meet Kâmil outside the *Vilayet* and proceed up the stairs to meet the waiting Governor.

Kâmil, as I have already indicated, was an extremely bright individual, who, without the benefit of much in the way of a formal education, could hold his own with all levels of authority. Early on in our relationship, we had both implicitly come to understand that we were linked by a symbiotic bond. Stated differently, we not only liked and needed each other, properly played we both had everything to gain and nothing to lose from our partnership. In my case, Kâmil was the interface between Hit *Bey* and the village (always managing to explain my strange behavior in such a manner that it became acceptable), and, as my popularity among the villagers grew, he took advantage of that fact and could frequently be heard saying "Hit *Bey* thinks we should do this or that, and, if we don't they are likely to take him away from us." This blackmail worked, and together we were able to complete a number of projects that alone neither of us would have been able to finesse.

The same was true in our relationship with the Governor. While he depended upon the *Muhtar* for periodic reports on my suspected 'spying activities,' he outwardly remained very friendly to me and never failed to enquire in the course of our weekly meeting as to what he could do to help my work. Kâmil, while on the one hand keeping me quietly informed as to the contents of his one-on-one meetings with the Governor (the topic of which was always queries as to what he had managed to learn about my real agenda), on the other prepared me in advance of each meeting with a list of items I should request from him in response to his weekly offers of assistance. In the course of the next year we both (and the residents of Bereketli) were to gain a lot from this relationship, but I never did get accustomed to getting up at 4 a.m. on a Saturday morning. When, after the 1965 elections, our Governor was replaced by someone who wasn't so interested in my doings, I almost came to miss our weekly get-together.

Chapter 12

The *International Herald Tribune*
goes up in smoke

A few weeks after I arrived in Bereketli I began to get the occasional letter from home. One of the first such to arrive was from my parents asking what I would like for Christmas that was just a few weeks away. I replied that I didn't really need anything but that I did miss reading the occasional newspaper. Some time later I received a notice from the *International Herald Tribune* office in Paris, informing me that I was the beneficiary of a year's gift subscription to the newspaper. Mail delivery to Bereketli was non-existent, all incoming communications were addressed to a *bakkal* (grocery store) in Balıkesir, owned by a man named Kemal from the neighboring village of Pamukçu, where whoever happened to be in town that day (if they remembered) would pick up any mail destined for the village.

In the normal course of events, Bereketli's communication with the outside world was provided by two competing vintage 1940s era buses. In theory both left for the city about 6 a.m. on weekdays and returned to the village around 4 p.m. In practice, both were seldom operative at the same time and if one had business in the capital you simply hoped that at least one would be running that day. On the days that both were in operation there was keen competition for customers

One of our two vintage buses

and the owners would make the rounds of the coffee houses before their departure to make sure that they had everyone aboard who might conceivably want to make the trip.

One bus was owned by Memdûh Aslantekin, the younger brother of the *Muhtar*, and the other by a certain Niyazi, the son of a family that had been deported to Bereketli following the abortive 1938-1939 uprising of the Dersim Kurds. When it was running, my preference was always the bus of the younger Aslantekin, who, given my relationship with his elder brother, was practically a member of my extended family. This did not sit too well with *Şoför* (driver) Niyazi, a rather surly individual, whose life had been marked by a number of stints in prison for a variety of misdemeanors and crimes, running the gamut from theft to attempted murder. And those were only the crimes for which he had been apprehended. At every opportunity he took it upon himself to display his displeasure with my preference for his competition.

After a while I began to realize that on those days when the only bus to make the trip to Balıkesir was that owned by Niyazi, I never seemed to get any mail, whereas on the days that Memdûh Aslantekin's bus made the trip, I frequently did. As the only piece of mail I expected on a more or less regular basis was the *International Herald Tribune*, I gradually became aware of the fact that I had never received so much as a single issue of my paper on the days when Memdûh's bus was not in running order.

I commented on this fact to the *Muhtar*, who, as always, promised to look into the matter. However, if my relationship with Niyazi was already strained, the *Muhtar*'s was downright hostile. Not only were the two families business competitors, they were also bitter political enemies, for Niyazi had been an active member of the *Demokrat Partisi,* and had even served a brief stint as *Muhtar* prior to the 1960 coup.

A couple of weeks later, on our return from the weekly visit to the Governor, Kâmil and I missed the truck we normally rode home in and were lucky to find another one that passed our village. No sooner had we taken our places next to the driver, than he, as was customary, offered us his tobacco pouch. When I opened it, I realized that the bits of paper from which we were expected to roll our cigarettes seemed better quality than usual. Upon closer examination I saw that this was indeed the case, and also realized that unlike the pieces of *Hürriyet* or *Cumhuriyet* (Turkish newspapers) that were normally used for this purpose, these particular bits of paper were covered in a language I could actually read and understand, and that the paper itself was a high-grade thin stock. Suddenly, the mystery of my missing *International Herald Tribunes* became apparent: they were being cut up and sold as cigarette papers. I pointed this out to Kâmil and he immediately enquired into where the driver had got his papers. He named a *büfe* (sundries stand) in Balıkesir where he had purchased them and the following weekend we made it a point to stop by and see if we could get to the bottom of this business. The *büfeci* immediately responded, "You ought to know, I'm buying these papers from Niyazi the bus driver in your village." The mystery was solved, and no sooner had we done so, than it was also resolved. Kâmil wisely chose not to task our larcenous Kurd over such a trivial matter (there were far bigger problems in the offing), and we simply stopped by the *bakkal* that served as our makeshift post office and informed its owner, Kemal, that in future all mail earmarked for Bereketli was only to be given to Memdûh.

After this I began to receive my daily newspaper on a more or less regular basis (if not quite daily). I did occasionally wonder just how much of what had been going on in the world I had missed out on due to my *International Herald Tribunes* having gone up in smoke. Thereafter, I quickly read each issue as it arrived, then cut up the paper into cigarette paper size bits and distributed them freely to one and all. The quality of the cigarettes smoked in Bereketli went up considerably, but the fact of the matter is that I was likely, albeit unknowingly at the time, contributing to a long-term increase in the village's cancer rate.

Chapter 13

A game of volleyball leads to my first confrontation in Bereketli

While neither the *Muhtar* or I had openly confronted *Şoför* Niyazi over his petty thievery, word that he had been the cause of my missing newspapers quickly spread through the village. It did little to improve the already less-than-sterling reputation of our bus-owning *şoför*. Indeed, were it not for the handgun he was known never to be without, he probably would have been ignored by all, for there was little doubt that during a short stint as *Muhtar* in the previous decade he had managed to put aside enough of the village funds to finance his current occupation as one of our two bus-owning entrepreneurs. Like most bullies, it was fear that allowed him to survive. Given his well-known criminal past, there was reason for caution in dealing with him. This was a lesson I was still to learn.

As mentioned earlier, one of the accessories I had been provided by my Peace Corps handlers was a package of sports equipment, that was designed to make me acceptable to the youth of the village. Among its contents was a volleyball and net. One afternoon, while engaged in a friendly game with a number of the village *delikanlıs*, I noticed Niyazi approaching. He strode onto the court across from me, pushing one of the boys aside, and announced that he was here to show us how to really play volleyball. I was unaware of the fact that after his last stint as a guest of the state he had returned to the village claiming to have been the star volleyball player on the prison team. All I saw was that with his arrival what had been a friendly little game had suddenly turned into a struggle of wills between an individual I already held in some disdain and myself. I should have walked away, but I too was young and a bit hot blooded, and I had no desire to appear weak in front of the young men with whom I was still trying to establish a rapport. For a few minutes the game continued, with Niyazi ignoring even the most elementary rules of the sport and generally acting like an ass. He argued every call and his boorish behavior not only spoiled what had been a nice afternoon for all, but he was clearly intimidating the players into whose midst he had inserted himself, and those on my side of the net as well.

After some time, I lost my patience and threw the ball to a boy waiting on the sideline and told him to take it back to the school where it was stored. That action had the effect of turning an already strained relationship into one of hatred on the part of Şoför Niyazi, who from that moment on viewed me as an enemy who had caused him to lose face. It was a childish action on my part, that only occurred because I was still upset about my missing newspapers. However, it was a reaction that was to have unpleasant long-term consequences.

Chapter 14

Pig's milk for the children of Bereketli

When we arrived in Turkey in the early Fall of 1964, the Peace Corps was primarily involved in providing English teachers for the country's middle schools (*orta okulları*). Our group was the first to break this pattern, as we were scheduled to be involved in something that the Peace Corps had virtually no experience in as yet: rural community development. Prior to our arrival, an agreement had been reached with the Ministry of Education, that included designating the thirty-plus villages (scattered throughout the width and breadth of Turkey) we were to be working in. In theory our activities were to be co-ordinated with the Adult Education Branch of the Ministry. I say 'in theory,' because in reality no one had any idea exactly what we were supposed to be doing.

The Peace Corps Director in Turkey was a man called Ross Pritchard, a former college professor from Memphis, Tennessee. Pritchard's previous claim to fame was the fact that he had unsuccessfully run for Congress as a Democrat in 1960, the year of Kennedy's election victory. It appeared to us that his reward for this failure in the political arena was his posting as the Peace Corps Director in Turkey. As events would soon establish, Pritchard viewed his new job as a stepping stone to what he clearly hoped would be bigger and better

CARE provides milk and bread for the children

appointments in the Kennedy administration. His approach was to convince his interlocutors in the Turkish government to allow more and more volunteers to come to Turkey. Given the fact that he knew absolutely nothing about the country or its customs, including the fact that out of politeness one never responds to a request with a direct no, rather you signal rejection by silence, Pritchard took the lack of a clear 'no' to his proposals for increasing the Peace Corps presence as acquiesce, and blithely continued to request new programs from Washington, all in hopes of enhancing his own reputation as a go-getter. The logic (such as it was) behind this approach was to draw attention to his activities in Washington by his leadership of what he was determined to build into one of the largest Peace Corps programs worldwide.

His ambition clearly outstripped both his own abilities, and the infrastructure at his disposal, and when our group arrived we found that the administration of our program had been sub-contracted out to a body called CARE International, a humanitarian organization known for its role in fighting global poverty. This body had rushed to put together some kind of staff (including a couple of volunteers from the first group to have served in Turkey who had just completed their two-year stint), who, time would show, knew no more about what we were supposed to be doing than we did. Prior to farming out the running of our group, CARE was known in Turkey as the body that supplied free flour and powdered milk to primary schools, a praiseworthy goal designed to supplement the diet of school children.

Shortly after my arrival in Bereketli I had a visit from a man named Jim Lebedeff, a CARE staff member from Izmir, who freely admitted he had no idea what he was supposed to be doing as my regional supervisor, but promised to provide all the free flour and powdered milk I needed, should we wish to have Bereketli included among the schools receiving this assistance. The *Muhtar*, who was present, quickly signaled his acceptance of this offer, and thus it was that a week later a truck pulled into the village, loaded with hundred pound bags of flour and large containers of powdered milk. The *Muhtar* quickly rounded up some volunteers and we transported the load from the truck into an empty room of the school house.

Within days, the schoolchildren of Bereketli were being provided a loaf of white bread and a liter of milk at midday, and, as this was our first project in the village, I began to feel that if this was what 'rural community development' was all about, maybe our presence in the village was going to work. These feelings were short lived however, as within a month word spread throughout the village that the powdered milk we were dispensing was actually *domuz sütü* (pig's milk). When I finished laughing at the idea of trying to milk a pig, I realized that for villagers who had never seen a pig and only knew that it and its imagined by-products were *haram* (forbidden by religion), this was a serious matter.

The *Muhtar* quickly traced the rumor back to its source, our village *Vaiz Hoca* (religious preacher), who had included an injunction against consuming this pig's milk in his previous Friday's sermon. The damage however was done. Soon only a handful of children were still drinking milk, and many had ceased eating the bread as well (it seems the rumor had included the equally false claim that we were mixing the powdered pig's milk with the flour used for the bread). After a couple of weeks of effort, during which the actual number of children participating shrank to a trickle, the free bread and milk project was allowed to die a natural death.

Not all was lost, however, as a couple of months later, the *Muhtar* and I found a willing buyer, for what little remained of our flour and powdered milk, in Balıkesir, and with the proceeds thus accrued were able to finance another project, namely, the construction of a fountain and pool in what we euphemistically called the village park, a small tree-covered plot of land adjacent to the village coffee house.

This was my first lesson in failure, though it would not be my last.

Chapter 15

A salary of $36.50 per month and no place to spend it

Our salary had been set at the princely sum of 327 Turkish *Lira* a month, a figure that at the then rate of exchange (9 TL = $1), worked out to be about $36.50 a month. When informed of this fact upon our arrival in Ankara, I remember thinking how in the world do they expect us to live on $1.25 a day? The rationale behind this amount turned out to be that it equaled the salary of a newly hired village school teacher, and, since we were going to be working with the local teachers, the powers that be had determined that we should receive the same recompense as our colleagues.

Soon after my arrival in Bereketli, I began to realize that far from being insufficient to meet my needs, the monthly stipends were beginning to accrue as I simply had no way of spending them. Not only was my lodging (the *Muhtar*'s office) provided free of charge, my meals (at least for the first four months) were also gratis. Likewise, for several months I was never allowed to pay for a cup of tea in any of the three coffee houses, let alone buy a round for the assembled body. As for the one and only *bakkal* (shop) in Bereketli, it too was owned by a relative of the *Muhtar*'s, and even if there been much to buy in it (there wasn't), my money was not accepted there either.

To make life even more complicated, we had been provided with what was euphemistically called a 'settling-in allowance' of $200 upon our arrival in Turkey, that more than covered the 'large ticket' items such as the portable radio, stove, kerosene lanterns, and, in time, a bed (which being elevated above the floor meant that the mice had to work a little harder to run over my face) and quilts. In short, my village needs were met and what little of my salary I managed to spend was expended in the course of my weekly visits to Balıkesir.

Indeed, my salary was such that it even covered the occasional mad foray away from Balıkesir. For some reason, the longer I stayed in Bereketli the more I began to dream about Chinese food. That particular cuisine had been a long-time favorite of mine and knowing that it was unavailable made it even more desirable. I had learned that there was one Chinese Restaurant in Turkey, the then newly opened *Çin Lokantası* on LaMartine Caddesi in Istanbul's Taksim district. The more I thought about it, the greater my craving for Chinese food, and the more I longed to try this place out. I found out that there were twice weekly round-trip flights from Balıkesir to Istanbul (on Tuesdays and Thursdays), and that a one-way fare cost just 30 TL, or roughly, $3.50.

Sometimes, those of us who can remember the Turkey of the 1960s forget that some things then were way ahead of where they are today. As a case in point we may cite the fact that forty-five years ago there were flights between a number of provincial capitals and the country's major urban centers that don't exist today. The Balıkesir-Istanbul run was one such.

Early one Tuesday morning, having become increasingly fixated with the idea of Chinese food, I took the bus from Bereketli to Balıkesir, having simply informed the *Muhtar* that I would be back on Thursday afternoon. At 11 a.m. I boarded the plane in Balıkesir (the window shades had to be drawn as the airport was a military site where a major radar installation was under construction), and less than an hour later landed at Istanbul's Yeşilköy Airport. My trip so far had cost a grand total of less than $4. I quickly boarded a waiting taxi and told the driver to take me to LaMartine Caddesi in Taksim, and less than twenty-five minutes later I was dropped in front of the long-anticipated *Çin Lokantası*. I walked down four steps and entered the half-basement restaurant and was greeted by the obsequious Yakar Çakar, head waiter and later part owner. Yakar *Bey* was the heart and soul of Turkey's first and, for many years to come, only Chinese restaurant. I ordered lunch and before leaving learned from Yakar *Bey* that they would reopen at 6 p.m. for dinner. Thus assured of my evening repast I walked across Taksim Square and checked into a room at the nearby *Otel Santral*.

Promptly at 6 p.m. I re-entered the *Çin Lokantası*, where, in addition to Yakar *Bey*, I was greeted by Doğan Wong, a co-owner, together with his mother and younger brother Kurban, and a silent Turkish partner, of what after only one visit had already become my favorite Istanbul haunt. Before leaving I enquired from my hosts at what time they would open the next day, and having been assured that they would do so promptly at 11:30 a.m., calculated that with luck I would have time for lunch and still be able to make my 1 p.m. return flight to Balıkesir. After a good night's sleep I returned to LaMartine in the morning just as the doors opened. A quick lunch of *çin boreği* (chinese egg rolls) and *soğanlı dana sötesi* (sautéed beef with onions), and a speedy taxi ride back to the airport, meant that at 2 p.m. I was back in Balıkesir with plenty of time to make the 4 p.m. village bus. It was a crazy thing to do, and it had cost me slightly less than a third of my month's salary, but my craving for Chinese food had been sated by my three meals in less than twenty-four hours, and, once again, I had managed to remind myself that there was indeed a world beyond the borders of Bereketli.

When later that evening I confided to Bonnie what I had done (as Peace Corps volunteers we were prohibited from leaving the provinces we worked in without permission from above), she had no trouble in understanding what had prompted my whirlwind visit to Istanbul, and made me promise that should I ever do so again I would include her as well.

Chapter 16

The Governor's shoes vs my *mest lastik*, or tables & chairs vs *yer sofra*s

Just as I began to think that my relationship with officialdom had begun to stabilize, one evening the return of the village *otobüs* brought word that the Governor was planning to pay us a visit the next day. Up until that point all of our meetings had taken place in the confines of his office, now we were going to meet in my new environment. The *Muhtar* was obviously not too happy about this unexpected intrusion and that night I was invited to join the *Ihtiyar Heyeti* (Council of Village Elders) for an extraordinary meeting to determine the manner in which we were going to entertain our guest. I say that I was 'invited' to join the meeting, but that is not really an accurate reflection of the situation. In actual fact, throughout the first year of my sojourn in Bereketli, I attended all the meetings of this august body for the simple reason that my lodging was in reality the village's *Muhtar Odası* (Mayor's Office), meaning that the Council of Elders' regular meeting site was my bedroom.

As the message from the Governor had said that he would be arriving just before noon, it was clear that he was going to be our guest for lunch. Likewise, he had made it clear that the real intent behind his visit was to see how Bonnie and I were adjusting to life in Bereketli, and that he was particularly interested in viewing my living accommodation. Bearing all of this in mind, it was decided that we would kill two birds with one stone and lunch would be served in my room. After some discussion about the menu it was decided that the Governor's visit warranted a chicken and as the *Muhtar*'s wife was particularly adept at the preparation of this dish, her services were volunteered by her husband.

The following morning was particularly cold, and while it wasn't snowing there was a particularly heavy rainfall of the kind that at any moment could turn white. I swept the floor and tidied my room, making sure that there was a basin of fresh water, soap and a clean towel on hand, should the Governor wish to wash before eating, and straightened the one bit of wall decoration I possessed, the photo of me standing next to Ismet *Paşa*, and then set out to the village coffee house to await our visitor. I was dressed as I always was in the village, complete with *kasket* (visored cap worn by village men), and *mest lastik* (my newly acquired leather footwear covered by goulashes), topped off with a heavy overcoat I had purchased in a surplus store before leaving the United States. I don't recall having given much thought to my attire, and, even if I had there was very little I could have done about it, as my only 'city' clothes, together with my only real pair of shoes, were in my closet-like hotel room, awaiting my next weekly visit to the Governor in Balıkesir.

I do remember that the mud was extremely heavy that day, and upon arriving at the coffee house I called over one of the young boys and asked if he would mind taking my *lastik* (goulashes) over to the nearby fountain and washing the mud off them. I was after all going to play host to the provincial Governor, the most important official ever to have paid a visit to Bereketli. He willingly complied, and, accompanied by the *Muhtar*, the village school teacher and the members of the *Ihtiyar Heyeti*, we sat down to await the arrival of our guest.

Shortly after, the long-anticipated car drove into the village square, and when the driver saw the condition of the mud surrounding the coffee house he stopped some thirty meters away from the door. He jumped out to open the car door for the Governor, who in due course emerged from the vehicle immaculately attired as always, and slowly made his way through four inches of mud to the packed coffee house. Those assembled jumped to their feet and shouted out *"Hoş geldiniz Vali Bey!"* (Welcome Vali *Bey!*) to which our guest, who was looking quickly around the room for me, mumbled a response. I, together with the men of the village, had removed my *kasket* as a sign of respect to our visitor, and when he spotted me standing next to the *Muhtar*, he marched over, grabbed it from my hand and waving it around said "What is this you're wearing?" I replied "That is my hat," and reached my hand forward to retrieve it. Instead of handing it to me, he dropped it on the floor, and, in so doing, spotted my shining *lastik* and the *mest* that they covered. He turned livid, and for a moment I thought that he was about to have a stroke. Instead, he motioned for a chair and sat down gesturing for me to take the seat across from him. After he regained his composure he said "What are those things on your feet?" Before I had a chance to answer he began a tirade, that, while seemingly directed at me, was clearly intended for all in attendance. The gist of his remarks, that went on for close to fifteen minutes, was that I had been brought at great expense (as if he had paid for my travel) from across the ocean ostensibly to teach these people to live like human beings rather than animals. Rather than setting the proper example for them, I had become one of them.

I, together with half the adult male inhabitants of Bereketli sat silently while he continued to berate me. In those years (I had just turned twenty-two), I was not known for my patience, and, indeed, I admit to having had a rather short fuse. Stifling my initial reaction to respond in like tone (fortunately my Turkish was still so elementary that I didn't have the ability to say what I wanted to), I contented myself with looking down first to my sparkling clean *mest lastik* and then turning my head and staring down at the *Vali*'s mud-covered dress shoes (the mud actually covered the bottom five centimeters of his suit pants as well). I did this not once, but over and over again. In a short time, every pair of eyes in the room (with the exception of the Governor's), began to follow my movements as I looked first at his muddy feet and then at my clean ones. My message was heard loud and clear by those in attendance and as I continued moving my head

Provincial officials visit Bereketli

back and forth between his filthy footwear and my clean ones, he finally realized what I was doing. He managed to regain his composure,
and asked me what I had to say for myself.

Mustering my best Turkish (by this time I probably had an active
vocabulary of close to 500 words), I began to speak in a very calm and
measured tone. I told him that while he was certainly correct that it
was my job to expose my hosts to how others lived, that I likewise had
come to learn from them. I continued that Turkish village life was a
new experience for me but that my hosts had been living it all their
lives, as had their ancestors before them. I pointed out that as long as
there were no paved streets and sidewalks in Bereketli there was going
to be mud, and that clearly the footwear known as *mest lastik* was better suited to this environment than any pair of shoes I might have
worn. I also pointed out that this particular form of foot covering was
far more affordable for villagers than manufactured shoes, most of
which would quickly fall to pieces and have to be replaced if ever subjected to the Bereketli winter. I concluded by saying that it was my

intention to continue learning from my hosts, who, when I had something to contribute with relevance to their lives, had already demonstrated their willingness to learn from me. When I finished speaking a deadly silence filled the room, punctured only by the slight nodding of heads. I knew that I had passed an important stage in my acceptance by the men of Bereketli. What I didn't know was whether or not I was going to have the opportunity to enjoy the trust thus engendered, or whether the Governor would use his near dictatorial power to have me removed from his jurisdiction on the next bus.

Some of the tension seemed to have left the room and for the next half hour or so we consumed several glasses of tea (coffee for the Governor), and chatted about such relatively safe topics as the weather (we were all in agreement that we were having a particularly nasty winter), and the likely prices of next year's crops. At some point, Bonnie joined our table and unaware of the discussion that preceded her entry, pointed to her own mud-covered shoes and began complaining about the difficulty of keeping one's footwear presentable in Bereketli. Once again, the faces of the men standing in a silent circle around our table broke into subtle smiles.

Finally, after what seemed an eternity, word came that our lunch was ready and we proceeded to walk the muddy two hundred meters that separated the mosque from the coffee house. I had previously explained to the *Vali* that there was no road his car could navigate, and that we would have to go on foot. When we entered the mosque courtyard, I and the other guests quickly washed the mud off our goulashes and then moved up the stairs behind the Governor who entered the room complete with muddy shoes, while the rest of us stopped outside the doorway to slip off our goulashes. I was surprised to see, in place of my *yer sofrası* (tray on the floor that served as my usual table), a real table and six chairs, that I later learned had been transplanted on the *Muhtar*'s instructions from the school house at the other end of the village, while the Governor and I were having our conversation. Kâmil Aslantekin had saved what was left of the day once again. Seeing our visitor's reaction to my *kasket* and *mest lastik*, he realized the likely explosion were the Governor asked to sit on the floor of my room for lunch, and while we talked had quietly directed one of his associates to gather some boys and have them bring a table and chairs from the school to my room.

As if this were not enough, he then proceeded to tell one of the greatest whoppers I had ever heard. It went something like this: "Until Hit *Bey* arrived in the village, everyone had eaten off *yer sofrası*. However, Hit *Bey* explained to us that this practice was unhygienic, and, as a result, the village carpenter was now swamped with orders for tables and chairs." I, and the other guests managed with some difficulty to refrain from laughing at this outright falsehood, but the Governor unaware of the deception to which he had fallen victim, congratulated me on my efforts, and repeated several times in the course of lunch that this was why I had been sent to Bereketli. Fortunately, for all of us, he never caught sight of my *yer sofrası* that was hanging on the wall behind him. Kâmil *Bey*'s wife Fatma had surpassed herself on the lunch, that even the Governor seemed to enjoy, and after finishing his second coffee took his leave and we walked him back to his car for the return to Balıkesir.

I learned later that evening from Kâmil that the Governor had taken him aside before he departed and ordered him in no uncertain terms to find alternative living arrangements for me, on the grounds that it was a bad example for the villagers to have the American living in the mosque compound. Our *Vali* was, as were all of the first-generation officials of the Turkish Republic, a staunch secularist, who clearly didn't feel at ease in the shadow of the minaret. I, however did, and no changes to my living arrangements resulted from the surprise visit of the Governor.

By the following Saturday he seemed to have forgotten the unfortunate beginning to his Bereketli visit, and congratulated both the *Muhtar* and me for the fine jobs we were doing. He would not have felt that way had he been in the village coffee house in the hours following his departure and overheard the tone of the discussion generated by his trip.

From that day on I was seen by the men of the village as one of their own, no longer part of the 'other,' but rather a fully fledged resident of Bereketli.

Chapter 17

Dominos, *pişti*, *altmış altı* & *tavla*: learning the rules

The clearest memories I have of that first winter in Bereketli are of the bone-chilling cold, and endless boredom. There was little I could do about the cold, as no matter how many layers of clothing I wore, it still found its way right down to my bones. To relieve the boredom there was the institution of the village coffee house. Given the cost of coffee, the name was a bit of a misnomer, as only on the rarest occasions was that particular beverage available. The three Bereketli coffee houses, as were tens of thousands of similar ones throughout the country's forty thousand villages, were really tea houses. Their menus began and ended with glasses of boiling hot tea, sweetened to the customer's taste with spoonfuls of sugar. The only choice one had was whether your tea was '*açık*' ('light'), or '*normal*,' that is with more or less water. With the arrival of summer, the coffee houses would sometimes add bottles of *gazoz* (soda pop) to their offerings, and then one had the choice of hot tea or a lukewarm soft drink.

In addition to tea, each of Bereketli's coffee houses had a battery-run portable radio, a *tavla* (backgammon) board or two, a set of brass dominos, and a few packs of well-thumbed playing cards. This meant that to relieve the boredom you had the option of listening to the

The *Muhtar* and I with friends in the coffee house

radio (that was only turned on for the periodic daily news broadcasts emanating from the state radio in Ankara), or learning to play some form of game. In my case I began with the radio.

In the winter months, one's social status determined the proximity you sat relative to the *soba* (small tin stove), and, as the American guest, I was always given the place of honor. This meant that I was seated alongside the stove, that during that first Winter always seemed to be burning brightly but never quite producing enough heat to assuage the cold.

No matter how many times a day I entered one or another of the local coffee houses the formula was always the same. I uttered the ritual *'selamünaleyküm'* ('peace be with you') and the assembled body responded with *'wa aleykümselam'* ('and peace be upon you'). This greeting was followed by those in attendance saying *'hoş geldiniz'* (welcome), to which I would reply: *'hoş bulduk'* (thank you). Then began a chorus of *'merhabalar'* (a collective 'hello'), that would likewise be responded to in kind. The only time this formula ever varied, was if I happened to be returning from a visit to the city, in that case the *'hoş geldiniz'* might be accompanied by a *'sefer geldiniz'* ('welcome back from your trip'). It was formulaic, it was ritualistic, but it was also heartfelt and very familiar. By the time the greetings ended a place had been cleared for me next to the *soba,* and as I sat down someone would invariably hand me their *tütünlük* (tobacco tin or pouch), a signal that I was to be his guest, and simultaneously nod to the *kahveci* that he should bring me a glass of tea. No matter how many times a day this process was repeated, it never varied in form, nor did I ever tire of both hearing and repeating the same phrases over and over. This became the clearest certainty of my life in Bereketli.

On most days, I would visit each of the three coffee houses at least once, and sometimes two or three times. My earliest visit usually coincided with Ankara Radio's first newscast of the day, and in the early stages of my stay in Bereketli, I did little more than pretend that I understood what was said. Fortunately for me, the major stories would invariably lead to a discussion among the listeners, and, generally by the time all had aired their views on the day's happenings I had some idea of what was being talked about.

By the time of the noon broadcast (the same news was repeated over and over at set times throughout the day), I could actually comprehend what was being talked about, and in the ensuing conversation, add my own two cents worth. By late afternoon, having now heard the same news at least four times, I was conversant with the topic of the day, and frequently found my opinion (as the representative of the outside world) being solicited. This was particularly true if the subject dealt with the United States, as it frequently did in the Fall and Winter of 1964. So often was I queried about why President Lyndon Johnson didn't like Turkey and why he had written his infamous letter warning that should it intervene militarily in Cyprus, the United States might not be on hand were Russia to take military action against Turkey, that I soon became fluent when it came to discussing the role of ethnic lobbies in the American political process. Much of my explanation fell on deaf ears as my listeners already knew that Johnson's attitudes *vis-à-vis* Greece and Turkey stemmed in their entirety from his wife being Greek!

In retrospect, I now realize that no matter how bored I may have been by hearing and discussing the same news item over and over each and every day, it was in so doing that I actually managed to learn some real Turkish, as distinct from the slang and profanity-laden patois spoken in the village.

When not listening to or discussing the daily news, I often turned to the only other form of boredom relief available in the coffee house: the games. I began with dominos, since this was the only game available that I had previously played (my maternal grandfather was a domino player and I had spent countless hours in his company as a child), and I felt fairly confident that I wouldn't embarrass myself. I was soon shocked to discover that no matter how hard I concentrated, I couldn't win so much as a single game, unless my kindly hosts allowed me to. After a couple of weeks of endless losing, I decided that there was something going on that I was not privy to, and began to pay closer attention not to the game, but rather to the dominos themselves. Sure enough, they were made of cast brass and had been used for decades, the result being that each and every tile had some distinctive mark or scratch on their back. These marks were clearly known to everyone but me and accounted for my theretofore failure. Without saying anything, I quickly mastered the tell-tale marking on three different sets of dominos (one in each coffee house), and thereafter impressed my fellow players with my newly acquired skill. Some time later (unbeknownst to anyone else) I switched the dominos in the village coffee house for those in that frequented by the members of the *Demokrat Partisi*, and thereafter seldom lost another game.

In time, I became equally proficient at the remainder of the available games, and the comradely banter, that sometimes included shouting, became one more feature of my new life in Bereketli. I would be less than candid were I to neglect to mention that the coffee house game tables (as had listening to the daily news broadcasts) had a noticeable effect on my Turkish vocabulary. For in countless hours of playing I learned to swear like a villager, a habit that in later years after moving to the city, I was to spend a great deal of time trying to undo.

Chapter 18

'But Hit *Bey* he's not a *Zenci* that's Ahmet *Ağa* from Çakırca *köyü*'

No matter how much time I spent in the coffee house discussing the daily news, there were some topics for which my growing vocabulary was still insufficient to explain to my interlocutors, in any meaningful manner, the nuances of the story. This was particularly true of one of the most widely reported stories of the time, the issue of race relations in the United States. I must have been asked a hundred times why Americans and, by implication myself, hated *Zenci*s (Blacks), and no matter how many different ways I tried to answer these queries I knew from the expressions on the faces of my questioners that I had failed to convince them. Often the question first asked was 'What is a *Zenci*?' followed by 'Why do you Americans hate them?' The issue of race relations in my native land, and the queries they generated in my new home, continued to plague me, and I spent a great deal of fruitless effort in trying to answer the never-ending series of questions they generated among my new friends.

All this came to a head, the day the *Muhtar* Kâmil and I were sitting in a coffee house in Balıkesir waiting for the Bereketli bus that was scheduled to pass by. At one point the door to the coffee house opened and in walked a black guy, in short, a living, breathing *Zenci*. I quietly turned to Kâmil and said "You and everyone else in the village are always asking me what a *Zenci* is, if you turn your head to the left you'll see the answer to your question just walked in through the door." Kâmil's eyes followed mine but there was no response. He turned back to me with a perplexed look and said "I don't see anything." I said, "Look, sitting alone at the table just to the left of the door." He looked again and then began laughing, "Hit, are you crazy, that's not a *Zenci*, that's Ahmet *Ağa* (Mister Ahmet) from Çakırca *köyü*." He then stood up and called out to Ahmet *Ağa* "Ahmet, Ahmet, come over here and let me introduce you to Hit *Bey*, our American." After the introductions, Kâmil turned back to Ahmet and said "There are some things I don't think I'm ever going to understand about our American. Do you know what he thought? He thought you were a *Zenci*." Then he turned back to me and repeated "Hit, Ahmet *Ağa*'s not a *Zenci*, he's not from Africa, he's from Çakırca *köyü*."

I had just had what was to be one of the most important lessons in my life. It didn't come from books, nor was it delivered by a professor. No, it came from the *Muhtar* of an isolated Turkish village with little more than a primary school education. He taught me one's appearance had absolutely nothing to do with one's identity. Who one is, was determined (in his framework) by where one lived and what one did, not by the color of one's skin. It was a humbling experience, but one that I have never forgotten. Even today, the lessons I learned that day in a smoke-filled Balıkesir coffee house make it difficult, if not impossible, for me to ever be comfortable referring to any of my fellow citizens as Black Americans.

I would like to say that this was the end of the story, but it wasn't. For the next few days I was forced to listen over and over again, as Kâmil repeated the experience with Ahmet *Ağa* to group after group of Bereketlians. I was the butt of a great deal of friendly laughter, that no one appreciated more than I.

A sequel to this story occurred several months later, when I was the recipient of a visit by Jesse Arnelle, one of the Peace Corps staff working out of the Ankara office. He was a former professional basketball player, who had won All-American honors in both basketball and football at Pennsylvania State University (if memory serves me correctly), and he was a big man (over two meters in height) with the largest hands I had ever shaken in my life. He was also black. When he unwound from the jeep that had conveyed him to Bereketli and entered the coffee house (where I just happened to be sitting), word quickly spread throughout the village that a friend of Hit *Bey*'s had arrived. Soon the room began to fill with men and boys, each of whom I introduced in turn to Jesse. I began to notice that some of the younger boys were getting back in line for a second introduction and that they seemed particularly interested in a repeat hand shake. Jesse, sensed this as well, and opened his right hand so that the boys could measure their own small hands against it. He was asked over and over again how he had ever gotten such large hands. By the time he left a few hours later, he had passed into Bereketli folklore, as 'Hit *Bey*'s friend with the giant hands.' Those hands remained a topic of conversation for some time in the coffee houses of Bereketli, but I never heard a single comment about his skin color.

Some months later I ran into Jesse Arnelle in the Ankara Peace Corps Offices and told him how his visit had quickly become part of the local lore. I also told him that all one ever talked about was the size of his hands, and that no one had ever asked about, or even mentioned, his skin color. He replied that this had been his experience wherever he traveled in Turkey.

Years later, after studying the Ottoman past, I came to the conclusion that the response of my Bereketli friends in both these instances may well be part of their imperial legacy. In Ottoman times, identity was based solely on one's religious affiliation. One was a Muslim or some variety of 'unbeliever.' Among Muslims, no distinctions were made between convert and native-born, nor were any made on the basis of ethnic or racial differences.

I would like to think that the lessons I learned about real identity while living in Bereketli have stayed with me throughout the past four decades. While, only one example of the many things I learned in my village life, no lesson was more important than learning that Ahmet *Ağa* was a villager from Çakırca, not a *Zenci*.

Chapter 19

Wine, laughter & the *Muhtar* in chains: Kuşkaya & camels

As the crow flies, Bereketli's closest neighbor was the village of Kuşkaya, that lay less than a mile to our southeast. In reality it was a good hour's walk away, as to get there one had to climb down the walls of a steep canyon, ford a stream (while passable in Summer was a raging torrent in the Winter), and then climb up the other side of the canyon. But it was far more than distance that separated the inhabitants of Bereketli and Kuşkaya.

We Bereketlians referred to ourselves as *yerli**, meaning indigenous or native, whereas the residents of our neighboring village were referred to by the term *Kızılbaş* (literally 'Red Head,' a derogatory

---

* Just what Bereketli's origins actually are is unclear: the earliest references I find to the toponym '*Bereketli*,' are in the 1940s. See: T.C. İçişleri Bakanlığı: *Türkiye'de Meskûn Yerler Kılavuzu*. Vol. I (Ankara, 1946), p. 150, where a village of '*Bereketli*' is shown as being located within the administrative sub-district of '*Konakpınar*.' Prior to that time, the settlement's name was *Mestavra,* a word whose etymology appears to be Greek, [Note: perhaps a contraction of 'meso' = middle, and 'stavros' = cross?]. In the Dahiliye Vekaleti's (Ministry of Interior's): *Köylerimiz*. Istanbul, 1928, p. 373, under the villages in the *Konakpınar Nahiyesi* (County of Konakpınar), there is a settlement called: '*Mastavra*'. See, also: Kâmil Su: *Balıkesir ve Civarında Yürük ve Türkmenler*. İstanbul, 1938, p. 147, footnote 1, where he identifies a settlement of the *Atcı Aşireti* (a *Türkmen*

term used by *Sunni* (Orthodox) Muslims to describe members of the heterodox *Alevi* sect. They were the only *Alevi* (*Kızılbaş*) village in our county, the other villages all being described (at least in Bereketli), as being either one or other of the two semi-nomadic groups known as *Yörük* and *Türkmen* (Turcoman). There were twenty-five villages in the Konakpınar administrative district, twenty-four of which had a village school, and a road of some kind leading in and out of them. The one exception to this rule was the *Kızılbaş* village of Kuşkaya, that had neither school nor road.

I had first visited our neighboring village when returning from a long hike in search of a lost sheep, shortly after my arrival in Bereketli. Turhan, the leader of our 'wild bloods', was on good terms with Arslan the *Muhtar* of Kuşkaya, and he had insisted that we stop by so that he could show off Bereketli's new American to his friend. I was immediately attracted to both the *Muhtar* and the villagers. Unlike my Bereketli hosts, wine was a staple in Kuşkaya and a visit always meant a glass or two of barely potable red wine. Arslan himself was an imposing figure with a quiet dignity, that far overshadowed the fact that he had never received any formal education and was therefore, together with his entire electorate, illiterate.

A month or so after our first meeting, I saw Arslan again. This time he was handcuffed and in chains, and was being led through our village by two of the *jandarmas* (gendarmes) from the county seat Konakpınar. His captors stopped by the coffee house for a cup of tea and we all began to query our unintended visitor as to what the problem was. It seemed that he was being transported to Balıkesir for having failed to respond to a written summons that had been sent to Kuşkaya from the capital. Seemingly unhampered by his fetters, he quietly sipped his tea, and explained that as neither he nor anyone else

---

tribal group), as being in the vicinity of the village of *Mestavra*, that, he states, is today's *Bereketli*. While I recall villagers using the name *Mestavra/Mastavra* on occasion, I don't recollect ever hearing an explanation about where it may have come from. As early as 1530 there is a village named '*Mastavra*' [sic. '*Mestavra*'], shown as attached to the administrative sub-district (*nahiye*) of Baş-girdek in Balıkesir. See: T.C. Başbakanlık Devlet Arşivleri Genel Müdürlüğü – Osmanlı Arşivi Daire Başkanlığı: *166 Numaralı Muhâsebe-i Vilâyet-i Anadolu Defteri (937/1530). [Dizin ve Tıpkıbasım]* Ankara, 1995, p. 252.

in the village could read, that such papers always went unanswered. This was clearly not the first time he had been carted off to Balıkesir by the local constabulary.

I asked how long he expected to be away and he shrugged and replied "No more than a day or two." I asked him to make sure that he asked for me upon his return, and, given the fact that the only route to the roadless Kuşkaya was via Bereketli, he agreed.

Later that day I asked *Muhtar* Kâmil if there wasn't something we could do to help Arslan's predicament. I did so, having sensed that the two men were, if not friends, well acquainted and genuinely seemed to respect one another. Kâmil said he just didn't see what could be done. I responded that, if Arslan was willing, we might suggest that whenever a written communication arrived from the *Vilayet*, he bring it to Bereketli, and we could read it an appropriate answer. Upon this suggestion, Kamil did not indicate an unwillingness to do so.

Thereafter, once a month or so I would have a visit from Arslan. At first, the inadequacy of my own Turkish meant that I had to find others to help figure out just what it was that he was being requested to do, but as my Turkish improved, I began playing a more active role in serving as his channel of communication with officialdom.

In time I learned that it was the proximity of Kuşkaya to Bereketli that was being used as an excuse for failing to provide the far smaller settlement with its own elementary school. That is, whenever they petitioned for such, they were told that they should send their children to Bereketli. This, despite the fact that several of the villages in our district that were even smaller than Kuşkaya had their own schools. The problem with this suggestion was that during the winter months the bridgeless stream that served as their only outlet (via Bereketli) to the world was transformed into a raging torrent, and there was simply no way the children of Kuşkaya (even had they been willing to walk the distance separating us) could have done so during much of the school year.

The answer seemed simple enough to me and I proposed to *Muhtar* Kâmil that we find houses in the village who would be willing to host the students from Kuşkaya should the weather and water level in the stream prevent them from coming and going. This rather naïve suggestion on my part overlooked a number of factors. Firstly, there was not a single family in Bereketli who was willing to host the children of people whom they considered to be heretics (the *Alevis* were widely believed, by their *Sunni* neighbors, to engage in a variety of immoral activities, the most harmless of which was the consumption of alcohol). Secondly, even had such a host been found, the villagers would never have countenanced their daughters attending class and socializing with boys from Kuşkaya. Gradually, I began to realize that there was no simple solution to our problem. When I announced my intention of going once a week to Kuşkaya and providing a basic literacy course for any residents who expressed a desire to learn to read and write, for the first time I found myself arrayed against the wishes of the entire population of Bereketli. It soon became apparent that while many of my new friends seemed genuinely sympathetic to their neighbors' plight, there simply was no way they were going to allow their American to make regular trips to Kuşkaya. Sensing their determination, I gave up on the idea. This was my second taste of failure.

I did however (over the objections of Kâmil), raise the issue with our friend the Governor on more than one occasion, and pointed out to him that there had to be something wrong with a policy that failed to provide the means of learning to read and write to a segment of its population, and then repeatedly jailed their elected leader for not responding to written communications.

His response was to order that henceforth all messages destined for Kuşkaya were to be sent to Bereketli, and as if our overworked and underpaid *Muhtar* (his salary was 100 TL or $11 per month) did not have enough work of his own, he was now burdened (thanks to his American guest) with the additional assignment of serving as scribe for our *Alevi* neighbors. As always, he acquiesced, and as time passed even commented on more than one occasion that helping one's neighbor was really a *sevap* (meritorious deed). While having failed to really resolve the underlying problem, I at least did not have to watch the *Muhtar* Arslan led about in fetters during the remainder of my time in Bereketli.

Me on a camel in my *mest lastik*

I was never all that certain how the residents of Kuşkaya (Bird Cliff) made their living. They had little in the way of fields, and the village might just as well have been named Taşkaya (Rocky Cliff), as the general impression it generated was of nothing but stone. That is not quite accurate, as it was also home to a large population of camels. It was this fact that kept me from enquiring too closely as to just how the residents made their livings, because I had already learned that camels were generally associated with smuggling and the moving of contraband goods.

However, in my all-too-infrequent visits to Kuşkaya, I learned a lot about camels from *Muhtar* Arslan, and for some time even gave serious thought to purchasing one of his animals, as a means of getting around the Peace Corps' ban on volunteers owning motor vehicles. I envisioned myself riding about the hills on a camel, until the day that Arslan and I actually began to negotiate a price. Only then, did he ask me what I intended to do with my purchase. I replied "Ride it, of course," to which he shook his head and patiently explained that in

Turkey one did not ride camels, you led them in a train from the back of a donkey. He went on to explain that the camel I was interested in buying was only five years old, and that meant that there were still two years to wait before it could even be trained as a pack animal. The upside to all of this was that if I still wanted to buy the useless beast, he would guarantee me that he would buy it back from me for a substantially higher sum two years later when I left. In other words, I was going to have the pleasure of paying for the feed and looking after a rather vicious animal (camels get extremely mean during the cold winter months) for two years and not get any use out of him whatsoever. I thanked him for his most generous offer, that I declined, and we parted friends.

Chapter 20

Hunting for *tavşans, kekliks* & stones

For the men and boys of Bereketli one of the few ways of breaking the monotony of the Winter months was hunting. For some reason unknown to me, this particular activity always occurred on Sunday, even though it might as well have transpired on any other day of the week, for during the late Fall and Winter no one really worked at all. Hunting in Bereketli, as in many other parts of the world, was inextricably linked to the passage to manhood, that meant that proficiency with a shotgun (there were and are no rifles allowed in Turkish villages, except those carried by the local constabulary, the gendarmes), was a must, and my new friends were particularly eager to see how their American measured up.

As a native of Oregon, I came from a long line of hunters, and while growing up had hunted for deer and elk with relatives. As such, I didn't feel any particular need to demonstrate my prowess with a shotgun, but during my time in the village no Sunday hunt was ever contemplated unless I was a member of the party. Our choice of game was limited to *tavşan* (jack rabbits), *keklik* (red-necked partridges), with the occasional *tilki* (fox) and *yabani domuz* (wild boar) thrown in for good measure. The first two kinds of game were shot for food, while the foxes and wild boars were considered nuisances, who preyed on chickens and cultivated fields respectively, and were simply shot as a public service.

Etiquette demanded that the successful hunter or hunters, as the case might be, host, for their less successful companions, a *bulgur* (cracked wheat) or *pirinç* (rice) *pilav* topped with that day's game (rabbit or partridge), an exercise that gave the hosts ample opportunity for bragging rights and made the guests the subject of gentle banter over their failure to bring home any food for the dinner party.

There were a few aspects of our weekly Sunday hunts that I didn't really enjoy. First and foremost was the size of the group; often we were as many as twenty to thirty men and boys. Second was the fact that custom dictated that we move forward in a line spread out across several hundred meters. I quickly realized that given the rough terrain we were hunting in, it was impossible to keep any order in the line and on more than one occasion, having flushed a bird or rabbit, I had to stop myself from shooting for fear of hitting one of my companions. If this was the case with me, I reasoned that it was the same for my fellow hunters, and in the same manner that I had no desire to shoot anyone, I had no particular desire to be shot. To lessen the risk of an unfortunate accident, I tended to fall back in the line that also had the effect of limiting the likelihood of flushing any game. It seemed to me that discretion was certainly the better part of valor in this situation.

After the first two or three excursions, during which I hadn't fired a shot, I began to be made the butt of gentle ribbing about my prowess (or lack thereof) as a hunter. As we returned to the village after yet another 'shot-less' afternoon on my part, some of the younger men began picking up stones that they threw as far as they could and then fired their shotguns in an attempt to shatter them before they hit the ground. This generally fruitless exercise went on for sometime, and finally the pressure grew for me to take a turn. Turhan, a close friend, and the leader of the village *delikanlı*s (young unmarried men), who likewise enjoyed the reputation of being the village champion at this particular pastime, was particularly insistent that I take my shot. Realizing that nothing would stop the clamor short of me actually firing my borrowed shotgun, I acquiesced, and Turhan, desirous of maintaining his position as chief 'rock splitter,' picked up a particularly small stone and threw it as far as he could. Instinctively I raised my gun and fired and wonder of wonders watched as the rapidly disappearing rock disintegrated into a cloud of dust. The appreciative 'oohs' and 'aahs' that accompanied this bit of blind luck told me that I had saved my reputation. From that time on, regardless of whether or not I had fired my gun, the walk back to the village always included a number of eye witness retellings of my proficiency with the shotgun.

Chapter 21

I am left holding the tobacco pouches

There were no police in Bereketli, nor for that matter were there in any other village in the country. Law enforcement in rural Turkey was (and still is) the prerogative of the gendarmerie (*jandarma*), a branch of the Turkish armed forces, that has a presence in each *nahiye* (county seat). As a *nahiye* is a sub-provincial administrative unit, composed of up to twenty-five villages, and a typical *jandarma karakol* (gendarme outpost), was commanded by a *Çavuş* (Sergeant) and some five or six conscripts (*ers*), there was no permanent police presence in Bereketli. Unless summoned in response to a violent death, about the only time one ever encountered the gendarmes was when they paid the occasional surprise visit in search of contraband.

In Bereketli and the other tobacco-growing villages of the *Konakpınar Nahiyesi*, contraband generally meant one thing: homegrown tobacco that had not (in keeping with the law's dictates) been sold to the state tobacco monopoly. Only when this was done, and it was appropriately processed, packaged and taxed, was one allowed to purchase it and roll it into cigarettes. Needless to say, this was a law completely ignored in Bereketli and all other tobacco-producing areas of the country. Indeed, the authorities seemed to implicitly accept the reality that this law was unenforceable, as the fines for being caught in possession of untaxed tobacco were relatively low.

No, the problem was not so much contraband tobacco, as it was smuggled cigarette papers. This is what the gendarmes periodically came in search of. This forbidden item was smuggled into Turkey from Syria in packages of one hundred papers, and the fine for being caught with them in your possession was a staggering 1 TL per cigarette paper. A hundred Turkish Lira was more than a month's income for the average family in Bereketli, and therefore, even if one had the means to use real cigarette papers (as I had taken to doing), instead of the bits of newspaper that were the preferred means, you never wanted to be found in possession of untaxed tobacco and you certainly didn't want to be apprehended with smuggled cigarette papers.

I recall well the first time I encountered a visit of the gendarmes. It was the middle of my first Winter and a large group of men were sitting in the coffee house watching a rather heavy snow fall when a young boy excitedly came bursting into our midst. I didn't fully understand at the time what he was saying, though I did pick up the fact that he had spotted a gendarme patrol heading into the village, and he had come to warn us that they were less than two minutes away. The villagers knew the drill: when the gendarmes entered the coffee house each man was required to stand to attention until they had been searched, and any tobacco and papers they happened to be carrying had been confiscated. There was no escaping this treatment if one were a villager. Indeed, there was only one person in the village of Bereketli who was viewed as exempt from such an intrusion. Suddenly, all eyes in the coffee house turned towards me. In unison every man was at my side pressing their *tütünlüks* (metal tobacco containers) inside my voluminous overcoat. No sooner had I secured the last of these unwanted offerings than the doors at both ends of the room burst open and everyone except the American visitor jumped to their feet in respectful attention.

In the next half hour, as one by one the villagers were searched, the *Çavuş* (Sergeant), who had joined me at my table next to the *soba*, and I had two or three glasses of tea. The tension in the room was palpable, and the level of frustration on the part of the gendarmes (most of whom themselves were village boys) became increasingly apparent as they uncovered not so much as a gram of forbidden tobacco, let alone any of the contraband papers.

Throughout all of this, I was visibly sweating, and it wasn't because the temperature in the coffee house had suddenly increased. I had begun to think about the fact that while it was one thing for me not to have risen upon the entry of the patrol, simple good manners dictated that I was going to have to stand when the Çavuş and his companions got ready to leave. I knew that were I to do so, well over a dozen tobacco cans would fall noisily to the floor. It was this thought that had led to my perspiration.

When the last search was completed, the Çavuş looked at me and carefully said "We are leaving now, but please don't get up." At that moment I realized the likelihood that either he or one of his men had been looking in the window when I had become the repository of Berekeli's combined contraband. I nodded in appreciation, and breathed a heavy sigh of relief as the door closed behind our visitors.

This experience with authority, as had the earlier visit by the Governor, taught me a crucial lesson. For the Anatolian villagers the presence of the state was something basically to be feared. I learned, as had countless earlier generations of Anatolian peasants, that when the government came calling it didn't do so bearing gifts. Government meant taxation and conscription, plus the occasional search for contraband.

Chapter 22

A night at the movies:
'Bell, Book & Candle'

I had already learned that the tempo and pace of village life was controlled by the seasons. Winter had now gradually given way to Spring, and the men, who throughout the past four months had spent their time in the coffee houses, now began to prepare their fields for the planting of that year's crops. As the first shoots of green began to poke their way skyward and the surrounding hills began to come alive, so too did I begin to feel the need for action.

Indeed, as what had begun to seem like a never-ending Winter finally began to draw to a close, and the mud that I had begun to loathe dried up, there seemed to be a general feeling that we needed to do something different. One afternoon, sitting in the coffee house, someone suggested that we should go into the city and see a movie. Memdûh volunteered the services of his bus, and I offered to pay for the movie tickets, an offer that would have been rejected out of hand a few months earlier and was now at least considered for a moment before being rejected. In a short amount of time we managed to gather twenty-five willing accomplices and without further ado piled into our vintage chariot and set off for Balıkesir.

When we arrived in the capital we discovered that there were two

Turkish films and one Hollywood production playing. My advice was solicited as to which we should see, and I (as events would prove), unwisely, opted for the American production that starred James Stewart, Kim Novak and Jack Lemmon. I had never heard of the film 'Bell, Book and Candle,' but, as I liked the cast, my recommendation was accepted, and in anticipation of seeing a light comedy, we dutifully purchased our tickets and entered the movie theater. No sooner had the lights dimmed and the film began than I knew I had made a terrible mistake. I've forgotten the scenario (or erased it from my mind), but I will never forget that the film dealt with 'warlocks' and 'witches' in Manhattan, two character types that were equally unfamiliar to the villagers and to the individual (me) they were counting on to make some sense out of what for all of us was incomprehensible drivel. It didn't help that whoever had dubbed the film in Turkish also had no idea of what they were doing, the result being that what we were hearing had little or nothing to do with what was being screened.

We were fortunate that it was a Tuesday evening, and aside from our rather ferocious looking group of twenty-five unshaven villagers, there were only a handful of others in the audience. When my companions turned to me and began enquiring in rather loud voices as to just what the hell was going on, our fellow patrons who were just as confused as we were, instead of telling us to shut up, began listening to our conversation in hopes of gaining a bit of edification themselves.

My problems were twofold. On the one hand, the film was indeed badly dubbed, and I couldn't make much sense out of the Turkish dialogue, while, on the other, I could figure out just enough from the action on the screen to realize that there was no way I was going to be able to explain the goings on of 'witches' and their male counterparts, 'warlocks' to my fellow movie-goers. I decided on the next best course of action and began making up my own plot and dialogue to accompany it. Needless to say, my version bore no relationship whatsoever to the actual film, but I seemed to be the only one in the theater who was aware of that fact, so for the next hour and a half I spun my own scenario and tried with my, by then, seven hundred and fifty words of Turkish to share it with the audience. Finally, the miserable film ended and we trooped out of the theater wishing that we were already safely home in bed in Bereketli.

It didn't help that this was the first film several of our group had ever seen, nor that we had had to park our *otobüs* a good kilometer from the center of town where the movie theater was located. For no sooner did we set foot out of the door of the theater than Winter chose to grace us with a final parting rain storm, and by the time we got to the bus we were all soaked to the skin. Nobody felt up to completing our planned program that had called for post-movie *köfte* (meat ball) sandwiches at an open-air stand along the highway leading out of the city (the only part of the evening's entertainment that by previous agreement I was to be allowed to pay for), and by general consensus we opted to make a run for the safety of home.

Unfortunately, the weather had other things in store. As we approached the stream that cut across the road some three kilometers below the village (just beyond the village of Taşköy), the torrential downpour had turned what had been a trickle of water when we left into a raging torrent. Memdûh refused to risk his livelihood by continuing on, and a silent convoy of twenty-five very wet and very tired, not to mention disappointed, men walked the final three kilometers back to Bereketli. It was weather fit only for witches and warlocks.

If there was an upside to this disastrous evening (for which I at least blamed myself), it was that I was so eloquent in our next Saturday's meeting with the Governor, in making the case for completion of the bridge whose construction had begun a decade earlier and then been halted 'temporarily' for lack of funds, that he finally took note and promised to complete the project. Something, to the surprise of us all he actually did do, and one unintended side effect of our night at the picture show was that within a couple of months one no longer had to ford the creek, but instead drove over a new concrete bridge.

The true lesson however, was a driving home of the reality of what I had been living with for the past six months, namely, that there are some cultural divides too wide to bridge without a great deal of hard work and preparation. Our night at the movies drove this lesson home in spades.

Periodically, throughout the next year, someone who had shared the saga of the night at the movies would ask me "Hit *Bey,* what did it mean when this or that happened in the movie we went to see?" Given the fact that these queries were addressed to the *de facto* screenwriter, I always had an answer.

Chapter 23

As Winter ended the rhythm of life began to change: the day we planted 400 *Kavak ağaç fidanları* (poplar seedlings)

B uoyed up by our success with the bridge, the *Muhtar* and I drew up a list of projects prior to each of our Saturday meetings with the Governor and spent many hours during the week deciding the proper manner in which we should approach him. One thing that Bereketli suffered from was a lack of available wood for construction, so we decided that at the earliest opportunity I should request several hundred poplar tree seedlings (*Kavak ağaç fidanları*), that we would plant along the banks of a small stream near the village. The idea being that this particular tree was fast growing and within twenty years would provide a timber source for village building projects. Kâmil and I were into long-term planning. This was partly due to the fact that we were both convinced of the futility of getting much done in the short term (we viewed the bridge as a miracle).

His pessimism stemmed from the reality that he was an appointed official who belonged to the minority Republican People's Party, that was not expected to do well in the elections scheduled for later in the year. In the short term, however, his weakness was also his strength. For all the provincial Governors shared his political affiliation and were desirous of doing what they could to ensure the success of the cadre of village *Muhtar*s who had been appointed (and were still serving) following the 1960 military coup. My presence, and the close relationship that had developed between us, was also a plus, in that the overwhelming majority of the villagers were proud of 'their American,' and therefore generally willing to co-operate in projects that I was associated with. At least that is what I thought. However, the issue of the poplar tree seedlings was about to prove the truth of the old Turkish adage *Evdeki hesap çarşıya uymaz* (The accounts we make at home don't work out in the marketplace).

As we were both convinced that even the most partisan villager in Bereketli could not help but realize the benefit of having our own village grove of poplar trees, we decided that this project would top our list of requests from the Governor. On the following Saturday the Governor listened to our proposal, and, while making no promises, did say that the official in charge of the state nursery where our hoped-for seedlings were currently residing was a personal friend, and he would see what he could do. He pointed out that even if he were successful there could still be a logistics problem as the office with the trucks that would deliver our seedlings was under the control of another branch of the government.

We left the meeting in a positive mood, and when we returned to the village walked down to the stream where one day we hoped to see a grove of poplar trees. Two months passed by with no word of our longed-for seedlings, and I had almost forgotten the matter, when one day a boy came running up to my door with word that three trucks filled with trees had arrived in the village and that their drivers were asking for the American. It was a hot day and by the time I arrived at the square next to the coffee house I was covered in perspiration. I climbed into one of the trucks and directed the driver to a spot on the road about a hundred meters from where we planned to plant the trees.

As fate would have it, the *Muhtar* had business in Balıkesir that day, and the *otobüs* belonging to *Şoför* Niyazi had broken down which meant that he was present in the village. Thus the one individual capable of getting our seedlings into the ground was away, and his political nemesis now had a golden opportunity to sabotage one of his projects. I wasn't worried about this yet, as I was more concerned about getting the seedlings out of the trucks. Getting them into the ground would come later.

The problem was that the three truck drivers had made it clear that they were simply there to deliver their loads, if I wanted their cargos it was up to me to get them out of the trucks. Alternatively, they were quite willing to return them to their place of origin. I pleaded for time and ran the kilometer back to the village in order to seek assistance. The men were in the fields, and the coffee houses held only a handful of the elderly men. School had ended for the year, so I managed to find a number of the older boys who expressed their willingness to help.

Together we managed to get the four hundred seedlings out of the trucks and then watched as the trucks headed back down the road leaving us standing with a lot of young trees that already looked like they were in need of water. Without saying anything else to my young helpers, who already looked exhausted, I picked up the first two seedlings and walked several hundred meters to the furthest point along the creek bed, to the spot that the *Muhtar* and I had predetermined our grove of trees would end. I set them down and returned for another load. Midway back to the road I met the first of my helpers, who, following my example, had likewise picked up two seedlings. He asked me where I wanted them and I told him to set them across the creek from where I had left the first two and that we would then work back towards the road on both sides of the creek.

By the time I got back up to the road, one of my young friends from the *delikanlı* coffee house had arrived and he began directing the younger boys to follow my example and start moving the seedlings down to the creek bed. The smallest of the boys was having trouble carrying even one tree and I suggested that he go back to the village and find me a shovel. He went running off and the strange procession of walking trees continued. They were about two meters in height and thus taller than any of the boys carrying them; indeed, the effect was of trees moving two by two down the creek bed as if they were actually walking.

As we were working our way back toward the road each trip got progressively (if not all that noticeably) shorter. I later learned that word had spread throughout the village and into the fields about our activity and a number of men had returned to the village to see what they could do to help. Upon arrival they were met by *Şoför* Niyazi who set about convincing as many people as he could that this project had nothing to do with the village, that it was just the 'corrupt *Muhtar*' who had used me to get himself a grove of free poplar trees, and that anyone with loyalty to the old *Demokrat Partisi* would be betraying their beliefs were they to help me plant the seedlings. Had anyone bothered to look, the ridiculousness of this lie would have become immediately apparent, for the spot we had chosen was on land owned collectively by the village. But for the moment, no one came out to see what was actually going on.

A couple of hours had now passed and most of the seedlings were in place next to where they were to be planted. I had received my shovel and started planting the first of the four hundred waiting trees. In the meantime, one of the boys had brought a jug from the village, and as there was a nearby fountain, we at least had something to drink. By others' reckoning I planted some thirty-seven trees that long afternoon. I wasn't counting. I do recall that at some point the other village bus carrying the returning *Muhtar* arrived, and shortly after, my ordeal ended. Kâmil insisted that I get into the bus and accompany him back to the village, a request I was only too willing to comply with. Using my bleeding hands and dirt-streaked face as incentive he quickly shamed the crowd of village men who had gathered round us and within minutes there was a stream of shovel-bearing men heading down the road to the waiting seedlings. In less than an hour they returned having made short work of finishing the job their American and a handful of school boys had begun.

One villager who was conspicuous by his absence was the village *Vaiz Hoca* (Muslim Preacher), a fact that particularly stuck in the craw of our *Muhtar* Kâmil, who thereafter never missed an opportunity to tell anyone who would listen, about the fact that while Hit *Bey* was planting trees "Our *Vaiz Hoca,* who was always preaching about how the planting of trees was a meritorious act, did not deign to make an appearance and help with our efforts."

Unlike the issue of my purloined copies of the *International Herald Tribune,* my second indirect confrontation with Şoför Niyazi was to have far more serious repercussions. By that evening we learned that he had actually threatened some of the village men with the illegal handgun he was known to carry, when they had attempted to come to my aid. This was not only considered a serious breach of acceptable behavior, it was also seen as a direct challenge to the authority of the *Muhtar.* Tension was building just below the surface and I was soon to learn just how dangerous life in a Turkish village could become.

Chapter 24

The *Muhtar* & I in Ankara

I had been living in the *Muhtar* Kâmil's world for almost a year, when I received an invitation from the Peace Corps office in Ankara asking both of us (and Bonnie) to spend a week on the Middle East Technical University campus, assisting with the training of a second group of rural community volunteers, whose program was being held in the deserted village of Yalancak. It had recently been vacated due to its location on land that had been set aside for the new university.

Partly based on our group's consensus assessment that our own training had been largely worthless, someone had decided that the second such group could benefit from actually undergoing their training on site in a real (albeit deserted) Turkish village. Likewise, they might gain some insight into what their next two years would involve by actually seeing how selected members of our group interacted with the *Muhtar*s in the villages we were already working in.

Kâmil eagerly accepted the invitation and we set off together for what was to be his first visit to his nation's capital. I didn't realize it at first, but even before the train pulled into the station at Ankara, I had become aware of an interesting fact. Namely, the tables had suddenly been reversed, and, I, the innocent in Bereketli, who had been so

Balıkesir train station: Bonnie and I en route to Ankara

patiently tutored by the *Muhtar* throughout the previous year, had suddenly become the teacher. Now we had entered, what was for my friend, the alien world of the city, where he was truly a novice, and I was back in an environment with which I was more or less familiar. Kâmil whom, as I have previously noted, was extremely perceptive seemed to take a delight in the changed circumstances and willingly deferred to my urban expertise at every turn.

I first became conscious of his helplessness shortly after our arrival in the capital, when I took him to lunch at Ankara's first Italian-style pizza restaurant, in the heart of downtown Kızılay. As we entered the restaurant I began explaining that pizza was the Italian version of *lahmacun* (a kind of Turkish pizza made with meat, tomatoes and *pide*), that the two of us had eaten on numerous occasions in Balıkesir. Indeed, that was the reason I had chosen this particular site, I wanted something different, but I didn't want it to be all that different for my guest. He quickly figured out that the only really significant difference between what we were eating and the more familiar Turkish variety was the cheese on the pizza, an addition that seemed to meet with his approval. I explained that, while I ate pizza with my fingers most Turks used a knife and fork. After carefully examining our fellow patrons' eating habits, he opted to follow my example and we successfully navigated our way through his first big city meal.

It was after lunch that he indicated the need for a rest room and I pointed out the correct door, thinking that he wanted to wash his hands. He was absent for some time, and just as I began to wonder if his first city meal had caused a reaction similar to that that I had experienced after my first foray into the cuisine of Bereketli (namely a need to vomit), and, while I was considering going to offer my assistance, the door opened and he re-emerged. I enquired as to whether everything was alright, and in response he simply shook his head back and forth. I pushed on and he replied that everything was fine, but he wanted to know "Why in the world did they make you perch on top of those white seats to do your business?" I wasn't sure what he meant and he elaborated, saying "After I figured out that you had to climb up on top of the ceramic chair, I had a hard time keeping my balance." His culture shock at encountering his first *alafranga* toilet was no less than mine had been a year earlier, when he escorted me to my first hole in the ground. I, too, had more than a little trouble learning not to lose my balance.

There was less to adapt to when we arrived at the deserted village of Yalancak where we were scheduled to stay. It wasn't all that different from Bereketli, and being located far outside the hustle and bustle of the city, Kâmil immediately felt at home.

During the week we spent in Yalancak, my *Muhtar* was a great hit. He had already been through it all with me; and the advice he so generously bestowed upon his eager listeners was not only solid, but practical. Since their Turkish was as rudimentary as mine had been a year earlier, I served as the translator for all these exchanges and, using the prerogative thus accorded me, managed to get in my two cents worth as well. Kâmil, who had spent the previous several months translating and interpreting my rudimentary Turkish to the villagers, loved the idea that it was now me who was making his comments intelligible to the trainees.

Kemal Kurdaş, the president of the newly formed university, was very big into the planting of trees. He had set the goal, if memory serves me correctly, of planting no less than thirty thousand seedlings on the vast expanse of land set aside for the university. Every visitor to the new campus was handed a shovel and I, together with the *Muhtar*, did my share for the greening of the Middle East Technical University campus. The experience I had recently gained in Bereketli stood me well in this endeavor.

Our stay passed quickly, but not before Kâmil had become proficient in the use of those strange sit-down toilets and been subjected to a number of new food items each of which was unlike anything he had ever eaten before. Upon our return to the village, he never tired of regaling the assembled residents with an endless stream of tales about the strangeness of life in the big city.

Chapter 25

Ross Pritchard & Kemal Kurdaş
come up with a crazy idea

If ever an American and a Turk were cut from the same cloth, it was Ross Pritchard, the first Director of Peace Corps Turkey, and Kemal Kurdaş, the founder and first President of the Middle East Technical University. They were kindred spirits indeed, as each was a perfect example of the old adage *You can't see the forest for the trees*, only in their case it read *You can't see the trees for the forest*. Both men thought big and acted as if there was no downside to their tendency to completely ignore such things as planning and details, as they followed their dreams. It has generally been my experience that when you put two such visionaries together in the same room, all manner of unexpected results may happen. This is exactly what happened the day that Kemal Kurdaş invited Ross Pritchard to address a group of underclassmen at METU (Middle East Technical University).

As previously indicated, Pritchard's ambition far outweighed his abilities. Having consulted with no one, he got up before a large group of nineteen-year-old Turkish students and began delivering a Kennedy esque-type speech in which he challenged his young audience with "Ask not what your country can do for you, but what you can do for your country." He then went on to describe the Peace

Corps in glowing terms, and challenged his listeners to develop their own Turkish Peace Corps and begin participating in the development of their own country's forty thousand villages. Pritchard thought that those of us working in rural community development were the only real Peace Corps volunteers, a view shared by many of those in the Washington Peace Corps hierarchy, that is, by those that Pritchard was so eager to impress.

Had it ended there, disaster might have been averted, but he was followed to the podium by the equally (although far brighter) grand schemer Kemal Kurdaş, who picked up his challenge and asked for volunteers willing to spend part of their summer working with the American volunteers who were already serving in villages round Turkey. That was me and my colleagues he was talking about, but it never entered anyone's mind to consult with us first.

I first learned of this hair-brained scheme while in Ankara with the *Muhtar*, when I encountered Chuck Lasky, the CARE-Peace Corps director of our program. He asked me what kind of projects I had in mind for the two Turkish students who were scheduled to spend six weeks of the summer with me in Bereketli and I looked at him like he was crazy. He realized my puzzlement and said "Oh, of course you don't know about this yet as the letters just went out to you volunteers yesterday." He then proceeded to tell me about the great plan that had been cooked up by Pritchard and Kurdaş. I listened in stunned silence and then decided that there was nothing to be gained by bridling my tongue and laid into Lasky with a vengeance. I told him this was the stupidest thing I had ever heard and then began to explain my reasoning: a) the summer months were when villagers worked, i.e., the one time of the year when community projects were virtually impossible to implement, as the labor force, including men, women, and children, were busy in the fields; b) we volunteers had earned a month's summer leave and everyone in our group had plans to be traveling away from their villages at the very time that he was proposing we work with the young Turkish students; and c) the idea of sending first and second-year Turkish university students, none of whom had any experience in village life, was a recipe for disaster and could have serious negative implications for the Peace Corps' future in Turkey.

Little did I know just how correct my assessment would turn out to be. Of the young students sent to our villages, two were killed in car and bus accidents, and a third, convinced that the giant spiders in his room were about to eat him, took to running about the village with a large butcher knife threatening anyone who crossed his path. After he and his knife disrupted the evening prayers, and he informed the Peace Corps volunteer that he wanted a woman and the woman he wanted was the volunteer's wife, the police in the provincial capital were summoned and they carted him off. However, as tragic as these incidents were, the hair-brained scheme hatched in the fertile imaginations of Prichard and Kurdaş was in fact to become the first in a series of steps leading to the closing down of the Peace Corps program in Turkey.

Having finished my tirade, I paused and Lasky, somewhat shaken, said that he thought I was exaggerating the downside of this plan and he was sure that it would all work out just fine. At that point, I really exploded, and said "Of course it will for you, as always you will be sitting on your butt in Ankara, with no concern and little understanding of what it means to live and work in a village." Our relationship, already strained, did not improve as a result of my outburst.

Chapter 26

Al Edgell's PhD thesis: the beginning of the end for the Peace Corps in Turkey

Upon my return to Bereketli, I found not one, but two, strange pieces of mail awaiting me. The first was the anticipated letter notifying me that on such and such a date two students from METU (I've forgotten their names) would be arriving in Bereketli, as the first wave of what was envisaged as an indigenous Turkish Peace Corps. I was urged to develop a series of projects they could assist me with, and to find them a place to live, etc. As I had already vented my spleen in Ankara, over what I considered to be the downside of this idiotic plan, I simply set the letter aside.

Indeed, when I opened the second letter, I quickly forgot the first, as its contents were considerably more disturbing. It was a letter from one of the CARE-Peace Corps staff, a man named Al Edgell. He was in my experience the best of the lot. He had impressed me (and others in our group) as a sympathetic listener, with a great deal of experience in international relief work round the globe; and, to top it off, he was an accomplished jazz saxophonist, a trait that particularly endeared him to me. A friendly giant of a man, he had, since the day we arrived in Ankara, generally shown a sensitivity to our affairs that was noticeably lacking in the rest of the staff. The problem was not Al

Edgell, it was the letter he had sent out to every member of our group. It included a detailed twenty-page questionnaire about village life that we were asked to fill out and return at our earliest convenience.

I immediately understood the purpose behind this document, as Al had previously indicated to me his desire to get a PhD in Sociology or Anthropology, and it was apparent that this questionnaire was designed to provide him the raw research material out of which he hoped to write a thesis. The questions we were asked to respond to ran the gamut from 'a' to 'z,', and literally covered every feature of village life, including income distribution, political party affiliations, the presence of outlawed religious orders (*tarikat*s), growth and use of *haşiş* (hashish) and on and on. Due to the depth of my immersion into Bereketli life, I could have answered most of what he asked with no trouble, but it was immediately apparent that this was dynamite. I remember thinking that I hoped the Governor was not monitoring my mail, for if he was this letter alone would confirm the suspicions he had not always concealed as to there being a hidden agenda behind my activities. For, in truth, the Edgell questionnaire was almost a classic example of what had been considered intelligence gathering in the late nineteenth century. If one were unaware of its designer's real intent, i.e., the furtherance of his academic career, it would appear to anyone who saw it as part and parcel of a not-so-thinly disguised intelligence operation.

I ripped the bulky questionnaire into pieces and put it back into the envelope with a note expressing my views as to both the inappropriateness of such a form and the possible negative repercussions it could have for the Peace Corps in general were its contents ever to become public knowledge. I suggested to Edgell that he would be well advised to recall it at once. He did not choose to follow my advice.

Chapter 27

The Turkish press discovers the Peace Corps

Little did I realize just how well informed my fears would turn out to be. In time, the young students from METU duly arrived and, if we had suffered culture shock upon our arrival, their shock was virtually terminal. They had been offered no training whatsoever, except for a two-day orientation (that had consisted primarily of warnings about what not to eat), and to say that they were unprepared for what they were to experience would be a gross understatement.

In 1965, METU, as were most Turkish universities, was a hot-bed of leftist activity and most of those young men who answered the challenge laid down by Pritchard and Kurdaş fell into the ranks of university Marxists. They were idealistic and, understandably, a bit suspicious about just what it was we Americans were actually doing in the villages. They arrived in mid-summer at the height of the harvest season, to find the villages practically deserted. In Bereketli most of the peasants were even sleeping in their fields and gardens and there were evenings when the only occupants of the coffee houses were a handful of old men.

In short, there was nothing for them to do. Nor, much to their surprise, were there restaurants in Turkish villages, and even the basic task of finding something to eat was often a problem. It immediately became apparent to the American and Turkish volunteers alike, that no planning whatsoever had been undertaken by the Pritchard-Kurdaş duo, both of the individuals in question having been satisfied to define the forest, while remaining blithely unaware that it was made up of individual trees, each of which required at least some basic maintenance.

In desperation, a number of my colleagues had the same brilliant idea. Why not assign their young compatriots to filling out the questionnaire they had received a few weeks earlier? After all, the new arrivals did have one clear advantage over us, they were native speakers of Turkish and this would give them something to occupy their time with. Thus began what ultimately was to be the unraveling of the Peace Corps program in Turkey. Several of the Turkish students who were handed the Edgell questionnaire reacted exactly as I had, and a couple even sent copies to journalists of their acquaintance. It was not long before a series of articles began to appear in the Turkish press (if memory serves me correctly the first such appeared in *Akşam*), citing the questionnaire as proof of what was already suspected in many circles: the Peace Corps was a branch of American intelligence. These stories, fed by other reports from our Turkish counterparts, relating how none of the Americans were really doing anything to help the villages or their inhabitants anyway, found a resonance among a growing body of the Turkish body politic and, for the first time, a significant amount of negative attention began to be directed at the Peace Corps.

While in the next two years, a number of other incidents, including the second director's traffic accident, that tragically resulted in the death of a woman (and his subsequently being whisked out of the country), as well as a series of ill-conceived programs, that at one point resulted in a couple of hundred new volunteers with no jobs whatsoever, all added to the growing press crescendo calling for the closing of the Peace Corps programs. Ultimately, this clamor was to lead to a gradual phase-out of the program and by the beginning of the 1970s the Peace Corps in Turkey was no more.

Ironically, it was the cracks that first appeared with the Pritchard-Kurdaş fiasco, and the fall-out over the Edgell questionnaire, that ultimately culminated in the program's demise. As both of these events were directly related to our group (we were known as TURKEY V, in keeping with the fact that we were the fifth group of volunteers to arrive in the country), one could conclude that it was the ill-prepared 'rural community development' component of the Peace Corps agenda (the favorite program of both Ross Pritchard and the Washington bureaucracy), that ultimately was the program's undoing in Turkey.

Chapter 28

A village wedding becomes
a night to remember

Near the end of that summer there was a large wedding planned by one of the leading families in the village. Everyone was invited, and yet, as the appointed day neared, there was a noticeable tension in the air. For three consecutive days prior to the festivities, the *Muhtar* made the rounds of each of the coffee houses and repeatedly read a decision taken by the *Ihtiyar Heyeti* (Council of Elders), banning all handguns from the scheduled event. Repeated enquiries on my part did not result in my learning why he was expressing such concern. After all, handguns were already banned and yet everyone owned one and there were few village weddings where at some point in the festivities handguns were not emptied into the air. Kâmil, despite his reluctance, was clearly reticent to share the real reasons for his concern with me and I never considered the possibility that it might have something to do with me. The big day arrived and, as night fell, most of the village was arrayed round the square on chairs that had been brought from nearby homes and the coffee houses. *Lüks lambaları* (pressurized kerosene lamps) were lined up on several small tables, that likewise had appeared round the perimeter of the square, and they cast a rather strange and eerie aura of light. The gypsy

A wedding in Bereketli

musicians imported for the occasion began playing, but there was little dancing going on.

Earlier in the afternoon I had been invited by some of my younger friends to join them as they fortified themselves for the upcoming celebration. I was tempted to do so up until the moment that I realized the alcohol they planned to consume was nothing else than *mavi ispirto* (ethyl alcohol tinted blue), the same material we used to get our pressurized kerosene lamps to burn. I had already encountered one young man from a neighboring village who had been blinded as a result of *mavi ispirto*, and as I had no desire to experience a similar fate myself, or to be faced with friends who had, I prevailed upon the *delikanlıs* (wild bloods) to forego the pleasure of drinking, with the promise that before the next scheduled wedding party I would make sure to have something more appropriate available.

I had been seated on the side of the square nearest the *Muhtar*'s house and I realized that many of the men I was closest to in the village seemed to be standing nearby. At some point I happened to glance across the square and saw *Şoför* Niyazi standing on a chair with a gun in his hand. He raised it and emptied the chamber into the sky.

Before the echo of the last shot had faded all the men had guns in their hands and immediately thereafter all the lanterns in the square were doused and the entire village was plunged into total and absolute darkness. I suddenly felt my arms grabbed on both sides. The *Muhtar* appeared before me with a gun in his hand, accompanied by several other men, each of whom was similarly brandishing a hand gun. He told me to quietly go with the men beside me and, as we started to walk quickly in the direction of the mosque, I sensed that we were surrounded by a phalanx of several armed men. All carried shotguns, but their handguns were clearly visible in the waist bands of their pants. For some reason, I don't recall being afraid, or of even considering the possibility that any of the commotion had anything to do with me. As we moved quickly through the darkness I do remember thinking that the long-anticipated showdown between the *Muhtar* and his nemesis, *Şoför* Niyazi, had at last arrived.

It was only when we arrived at my room, and my guardians, rather than leaving, took up their positions throughout the mosque courtyard and arrayed themselves both inside and outside my room, that I began to really wonder what was going on. Throughout the night, the *Muhtar* Kâmil (always accompanied by other armed men) paid frequent visits and despite my growing insistence still refused to tell me what was going on. As the hours advanced, gunshots were occasionally heard from far away and on each such occasion my guards assumed an even more alert stance. Morning finally came, although I don't remember having ever gone to sleep. Someone brought breakfast and shortly before 10 a.m. the *Muhtar* arrived and with a few words dismissed the waiting men. They said their goodbyes and went home to what must have been some very anxious families.

Again I asked Kâmil what was going on and all he would say was that Niyazi had fled the village during the night and that the danger was now over. It was some time before I began to piece together the actual events of that strange evening. It seems that *Şoför* Niyazi had not only been openly bragging of his plans to disregard the handgun ban, but had also announced his intention of using the cover of the wedding to finally dispense with the *Muhtar* and his troublesome

Watching the village men dance at a wedding

American friend who had had the temerity to have shown him disrespect. While, like most blowhards, he was largely talk, the *Muhtar* wasn't about to risk having the blood of the village's American guest shed on his watch. Hence, the heightened security. What was most interesting about this event was the fact that all of the intelligence about Niyazi's threats came to the *Muhtar* from people who were considered to be the political allies of our now missing *şoför*.

When Niyazi disappeared so did his *otobüs* (it must have doubled as his getaway vehicle) and, while both were to return a month later, in the interim the inhabitants of Bereketli were totally dependent upon the equally ancient vehicle that was the pride and joy of Memdûh. On the days it was running we had contact with the outside world, when it was inoperative (as was often the case) we were confined to the village.

Chapter 29

Lessons learned in the *Muhtar Odası*: 'We like Ismet Inönü better this way in Bereketli'

Not only did I sleep and listen to the Voice of America's late-night Jazz Hour in the *Muhtar*'s office, I also had my introduction to the rough and tumble of Turkish politics, as played out at the village level, in that room. Anyone who feels that Turkish villagers do not keep up with what's going on in the country's political arena should have spent the months leading up to the 1965 General Elections in Bereketli. Day after day in the coffee houses and night after night in the *Muhtar Odası*, also known as my humble abode, the full saga of the country's political future was endlessly discussed.

No one had bothered to brief our group of Peace Corps volunteers on the fact that all of the *muhtars* we would be working with were members of the Republican People's Party, that is, the party of Atatürk, that was seen by all proponents of the coup-ousted Democratic Party of Adnan Menderes as the illegitimate holders of power. When we arrived in Turkey, I and my fellow volunteers (each of whom in order to accomplish anything were going to have to establish a rapport with the *muhtar* in our villages), were sent blindly out into the wilds of Anatolia without any idea of the quagmire we were stepping into.

At home in the *Muhtar Odası*

In my case, Bereketli was a village that had since the advent of multi-party elections, fifteen years earlier, cast a minimum of eighty percent of its votes in favor of the now dissolved *Demokrat Partisi*. As if the closing of their political voice was not bad enough, the military that had ousted Menderes in 1960, had ended up two years later putting the first freely elected leader of the young Turkish Republic on trial, and then to make matters worse, executed the former Prime Minister and two of his associates. As for the rest of his party's politicians, the men who had run the country in the decade of the 1950s, most of them were in prison, and those who weren't were banned from playing any role in the country's political future.

Most people in Bereketli (and throughout Menderes' home territory of western Anatolia as well), believed that the former general Ismet İnönü, the man I had met almost as soon as I set foot in Turkey, was the *eminence grise* behind the military's unpopular actions, and, at the very least, given the fact that he was now Prime Minister, their obvious beneficiary. I arrived in Bereketli unaware of any of this.

On my first trip into Balıkesir I had my photo of Ismet *Paşa* framed, and upon my return to the village proudly hung it on my wall above the fireplace, and, in so doing, also provided it a place of prominence in the Mayor's Office. While this did not bother the *Muhtar*, who was an Inönü partisan, it clearly did not sit all that well with the majority of his constituents who happened to have business there. Most, when I proudly showed them my prized photo, were far too polite to say anything. Not so, with the gangly village clown, known as *Hırsız* (Thief) Ibrahim. I seem to recall that the *'hırsız'* label may actually have been given him by myself, due to his propensity of picking up any item I left around (he was particularly fond of my ballpoint pens and cigarette lighters), but whatever its origin, it caught on quickly and soon everyone referred to him by that sobriquet. Despite, or perhaps because of, my labeling him in this manner, we soon became close friends and Ibrahim was the one man in Bereketli whom I could always depend on to tell me the truth. He pulled no punches when I did something stupid, or managed to offend the prevailing norms of propriety, he always made sure that I knew it.

Thus, it was no real surprise the evening he showed up to get a document signed by the *Muhtar*, and having spotted my picture of Inönü, he walked over to it and turned it face down against the wall. "Hit," he said, "you've been here long enough by now that you should know that in Bereketli we like Ismet *Paşa* better this way." From that day on the *Paşa* and I faced the wall! While this was one of my first lessons in local politics, it was not to be my last.

As the temperature leading up to the elections, that were scheduled to return Turkey's fragile democratic order, heated up candidates began (as they did prior to every election) paying attention to villagers, who, after all, did comprise no less than sixty percent of the electorate. This attention even managed to reach Bereketli and, in the weeks leading up to the election, a number of would-be parliamentarians dropped in to solicit votes. Wanting to ensure an audience, word was always sent out the day before they planned to visit, via the returning village *otobüs*.

As the village coffee house was in the *meydan*, directly adjacent to where our buses unloaded their passengers, word of the impending visit spread quickly, and a favorite pastime was provided by *Hırsız* Ibrahim, who, in anticipation of the next day's arrival, would mount a chair in the coffee house and regale us with the speech we were going to hear. Complete with the appropriate gestures he would bellow out the litany of empty promises that villagers throughout the country heard prior to each round of voting. After each such soliloquy I could hardly wait for the next day and, time after time, I heard the actual candidates repeat, often practically verbatim, what Ibrahim had regaled us with the previous evening.

The man was a comic genius, but that fact did little to lessen the sense of futility that I and everyone present felt when we heard the candidates mouthing the same empty promises day after day. The litany never varied, "If our party is elected, I guarantee that you will have a real road, electricity, a telephone, and water system before the end of the first year we are in power." Election after election, promise after promise, and neither the village road program, rural electrification, or water programs ever got beyond the level of what *Hırsız* Ibrahim so eloquently put as *boş lâflar* (hollow words). For he and the rest of the country's villagers were well versed in the meaning of the old Turkish proverb *'Boş lâf karın doyurmaz'* (Empty words do not fill the stomach).

Many years later, when I repeated this story to Turgut Özal (who was then President after having served two terms as Prime Minister), I added the fact that in my view one of the key reasons for his own early political success had been the fact that in his first term as Prime Minister (1983-1987), he had indeed fulfilled the empty promises that I had first heard in the Bereketli coffee house. He smiled and said, "Don't forget, growing up in small towns like Silifke and Söğüt in the 1930s, I too listened to an earlier generation of politicians making the same speech." While the urban centers of Turkey remained blithely unaware of the fact, Özal had indeed undertaken a massive development program on behalf of the country's rural inhabitants. When completed, virtually every village in the country did have a passable road, electricity, clean drinking water and a state-of-the-art pay telephone that served as a link with the outside world. I sometimes wonder what today's generation of politicians are promising the rural electorate.

Another factor in Özal's early success was the bi-weekly television program he instituted called '*Icraatin Içinden*' (Inside the Operations). With pen in hand, and accompanied by flow charts, he talked to the country about subjects like globalization and the free market economy. Most of my urban friends laughed at the idea of villagers listening to such talk, but Turgut *Bey* knew, just as I did, that the Turkish villager is a much more sophisticated being than they are credited with by their urban counterparts.

Chapter 30

I cast a vote for *Çoban Sülü*

A t last the long-awaited elections, that were set to spell the country's return to a democratically elected government, approached. In Bereketli (as throughout much of the country) the sentiments clearly favored the candidacy of a young engineer named Süleyman Demirel. Head of the newly formed *Adalet Partisi* (Justice Party), the not-so-well-concealed successor to the banned Democrat Party of the late Adnan Menderes, Demirel was quite willing to acknowledge his own village roots, and equally at home with the nickname: *Çoban Sülü* (Süleyman the Shepherd). Already he had learned to play the role of populist, a technique he was to elevate to unprecedented heights in a career spanning the next four decades, one that would see him serve seven times as Prime Minister and once as President (he too, as Menderes before him, was twice to be the subject of military *coup d'etats*, although, as of this writing, he has managed to escape the final indignity exacted on his spiritual predecessor).

The evening before the election a large group of us were sitting in the village coffee house, when the oldest man in the village, fondly known by one and all as Adnan *Dayı* (Uncle Adnan), spoke up. Due to the fact that he was virtually blind he spent a lot of time in the coffee house and we had become quite friendly. He seldom opened his mouth and when he did, partly out of deference to his age and partly due to the fact that on those rare occasions when he did say something, it was usually worth listening to, the room silenced. He began "You know I can't see anymore and you also know that I don't trust anyone from this village. In fact, there is only one person in Bereketli whom I do trust and that is our American Hit *Bey*. Therefore, tomorrow it is Hit *Bey* who is going to take me to the school house to cast my vote and it is he who is going to mark my ballot." No one said anything, and after a moment he continued, "Hit *Bey* is the only person I can be sure will vote for *Çoban Sülü* on my behalf." No one had the temerity to explain to the oldest living resident of Bereketli that it was more than a little irregular for an American to vote in a Turkish election and that is how I became the only foreigner to cast a vote in what turned out to be Demirel's most impressive political victory. The fifty-seven percent of the vote he garnered in the 1965 elections far outweighed anything he was to achieve vote wise in the next forty years.

Bright and early the next morning, I stopped by the coffee house and, with Adnan holding my arm in one hand and his ever-present cane in the other, we set off to walk the 200 meters to the school. We arrived and picked up Adnan *Dayı*'s ballot. I dutifully marked it in keeping with his instructions, folded and placed it in the ballot box and we returned to the coffee house.

Almost forty years later I related this anecdote to Süleyman Demirel, who had just completed his term as President. He smiled slightly, nodded as if thanking me for the vote, but made no further comment.

Chapter 31

I join the ranks of the married men

To this day I do not know how much of Jeanne and my decision to get married that summer stemmed from love and how much was a reflection of the sense of separateness and loneliness we both had been experiencing throughout the past nine months. I have a feeling that on my side, there was also an unspoken, indeed unconscious, desire to experience how my status in the village would be affected by taking, what by Bereketli standards, was the long overdue step of joining the ranks of the married men. In retrospect I do know, and my now ex-wife Jeanne concurs, that a decision on marriage is probably not best made while living in a village society other than one's own. The normal problems of adjustment to married life are greatly enhanced when one encounters them in the setting we found ourselves in. I, for my part, had just become accustomed to a lifestyle in which my waking hours were spent in the company of my fellow men and, in retrospect, I realize that I was blithely unaware of the need to adjust this behavior pattern in light of my new married status. After all, my contemporaries, the village men of Bereketli, didn't seem to spend all that much time at home either.

Given the fact that my new wife was by training and profession a registered nurse, that is qualified to provide the kind of medical advice

The 'doctor' examines a patient

that I had been gratuitously dispensing during the past twelve months, the part of my daily routine that had consisted of cleaning and bandaging a variety of cuts and bruises and telling my 'patients' that they had to see the doctor in Balıkesir was lifted from my shoulders. This meant that I had even more time to spend with the men of the village. As for my former peers, the unmarried *delikanlı* (wild bloods) of the village, they seemed to sense my changed status and no longer were so insistent that I join them in their coffee house or on hunting and fishing expeditions.

My transition to the status of married man was greatly facilitated by our new landlords. As there had been no question of the two of us occupying my bachelor quarters in the mosque courtyard, the *Muhtar* suggested that we move into the unoccupied finished room of a house belonging to Mehmet Sadık Demirel and his wife Meliha. As the Demirels were quite willing to share their dwelling, we did so, and before long had become close friends.

Mehmet Sadık was by trade a tailor who suffered from frequent crippling migraine headaches. When he worked, that was infrequently due to the fact that the action and noise of his treadle Singer sewing machine seemed to aggravate his medical condition, he was one of the fastest and finest tailors I have ever seen. He could measure a man for a suit, cut the cloth, and deliver a finished outfit in a matter of two or three hours. He, unlike most of the men in Bereketli, spent little time in the coffee houses and, as he was usually at home, became adept at assisting Jeanne (or Cini as she was called locally) in organizing and looking after the patients who lined up outside our door waiting for her ministrations. He ranked them by his own means as to the seriousness of their complaints, and, in the process, developed a real interest in looking after the ill. When the 'patients' from neighboring villages arrived at what he considered inopportune hours he was not above telling them that the price for a visit was 20 TL (a large sum by village standards) and sending them on their way. While he himself had neither the means nor possibility to develop this talent, I was not all that surprised when on a visit to Bereketli twenty-five years later, I learned that his daughter (born after our departure) and his son (a toddler when we were housemates) had both graduated from university and the daughter had become a doctor and the son a dentist. As I had already guessed (and he assured me), it was his own interest developed as Cini's assistant that led him to make great sacrifice and led to his children becoming the first Bereketli-born doctor and the first Bereketli-born dentist in the village's history.

If it was Cini's influence that led to his daughter's choice of medicine as a career, it may have been his own bad teeth (a trait I shared) that convinced him to push his son towards dentistry. I still remember with a grimace the day when seated next to each other on a low stone wall next to his house, we both lost teeth at the hands of the itinerant barber who visited the village periodically. I went first, because I had a feeling that if I saw how our barber-dentist operated, I wouldn't have the courage to continue. I closed my eyes to avoid looking as the 'dentist' extracted an infected molar with a pair of pliers. I grimaced with the pain, but when it was Mehmet Sadık's turn he sat stoically as the traveling dentist extracted not one, but two, of his teeth. He had the advantage over me in that from the gaps in his mouth it was clear that he had on several previous occasions made the acquaintance of our *dişçi* (dentist).

Chapter 32

We build a house: the changing face of Bereketli

The *Halk Eğitim Müdürlüğü* (Adult Education Directorate), a branch of the Ministry of Education, with whom I was nominally working during my time in Bereketli, had assigned two bright young teachers, Kemal Beyaz and Yusuf, to the village. Their job was to provide a one-year course in 'carpentry' and 'masonry' respectively to young boys who had finished their formal education (five years of primary school). During my first year I spent part of most days in their company and, while I had little to add to their efforts (being a middling carpenter at best and with no knowledge whatsoever of masonry), we became close friends and planned a number of projects together.

Relying upon my on–off relationship with the Governor, we drew up plans for a simple village house, one that would be both economical and far more practical than the traditional Bereketli residences that were two-story stone structures and that never seemed to be quite finished. When first built, only one upstairs room would be completed as the family's living quarters, with the remainder of the unfinished upstairs rooms set aside for storage, and the bottom floor used as a stable. In theory, when one's first son was married, a second upstairs

A local Bereketli house

room would be finished for the new couple. In practice, however, the custom was no longer observed and with the marriage of each son a new house, a carbon copy of the old, was built.

The downside to this style of architecture was obvious: while the animals that lived downstairs did generate some useful heat during the winter months, they were also the source of the countless fleas who loved nothing better than to relocate from their four-legged hosts downstairs to the two-legged ones who lived directly above them. In addition, the typical Bereketli house had no toilet or bathing facilities whatsoever (a hole in the ground at some distance from the house, that was surrounded by a low-lying wooden fence serving the purpose), and likewise did not possess much in the way of a practical fireplace, that is, one that could serve the dual function of family cooking stove and still provide a modicum of heat during the winter. Finally, by building a house that you only occupied a small portion of meant that you were engaging in a lot of wasted expense. To address this need, Kemal, Yusuf, and I drew up plans for a small, compact, four-room dwelling that could be heated by running stove pipes from both the fireplace and a *soba* through each of the four rooms. As an added bonus, one of the rooms was an indoor bathroom. Against one outside wall of the house we placed a stable for cattle and sheep, but in such a manner that its inhabitants would not be sharing their fleas with the family.

We made sure that everything to be used in the construction was available in the village and, by our calculations, the adoption of our plan would not only go a long way toward raising the quality and standard of life in the village, it would also save a considerable sum in construction costs. We were fully aware that explaining our plan was not going to convince anyone to try it. No, we needed a model house. We had the labor, as we intended for the actual construction to be carried out by our group of newly trained young carpenters and masons as a kind of graduation exercise, but we still needed a minimal sum of money to turn our dream into reality.

Once again, it was my on–off relationship with the provincial Governor, that we were banking on. Armed with a truly professional set of scaled drawings, that would have made any architect proud (Kemal and Yusuf were very good at their jobs), I was dispatched to Balıkesir to see if I could prevail upon the good graces of officialdom and extract a sum of about $250 to turn our dream into reality.

During my year in the village, I had actually come to admire (if not like) the Governor, who had quite clearly done all in his power to facilitate the *Muhtar* and my plans. On his part, I had begun to feel that he had finally decided that I might not actually be a spy (I never could figure out what it was that anyone could possibly be interested about spying on in Bereketli) and might even (despite my *kasket* and *mest lastik*) be capable of making some contribution to the 'civilizing' of my fellow villagers.

Nor in this, what was to be our last encounter, did he disappoint. He promised to find, if not money, a good part of what we needed, namely cement and bricks. He was true to his word and shortly thereafter Kemal, Yusuf, the students and I began work on what was to be the first new type of dwelling that Bereketli had seen in several hundred years.

Work progressed quickly and as the walls went up, more and more volunteer labor began to show up; in a matter of weeks the 'model house' was completed and ready for it first occupant. As I had declined the honor, it was decided that it would serve as the residence of the village school teacher, a logical step as it was located directly opposite the entrance to the school. Within a year, three more houses based on its design had sprung up in the village, although each had been modified in accordance with its owners needs.

Chapter 33

The camel gets a leg

We had only been in our new lodging for a short time, when I was woken early one morning by a piercing scream outside the window. I rushed out, just in time to see a camel shaking an old woman around like a rag doll. He had one of her legs in his mouth and seemed intent on tearing it from her body. I picked up a nearby stick and began to beat his head, just as his owner (one of my wood deliverymen) appeared. He grabbed the stick from my hand and began poking the camel in rather tender parts of his anatomy, an action that had the effect of causing him to lose his grip on the old woman who toppled to the ground. By this time nurse Cini had arrived on the scene and within minutes had gotten a tourniquet around the woman's thigh, an action that undoubtedly saved her life.

Attracted by her screams, other neighbors began to arrive and it was quickly determined that no one knew who the victim was. We later learned that she was from a neighboring village and had set out before dawn to take the 6 a.m. bus to Balıkesir for a visit to the doctor. We quickly carried her to the bus that was about to depart and, with Cini frequently loosening the tourniquet, managed to get her to the hospital in the provincial capital within an hour of the attack. Once again, it was my friend Dr Özcan *Bey* who happened to be on duty and he managed to save both the patient and her leg.

If my earlier failed efforts to save the life of the young mother, who had ingested the lethal dose of the oil of thyme, had contributed to my undeserved reputation as a healer, Cini's far more successful ministrations resulted in an even heavier flow of visitors to our door.

Chapter 34

Kan davası: cleaning up the nest of bastards (*piç yuvası*)

I don't really recall the exact point in time that I was made privy to the dark secret that festered like a canker under the smooth exterior of life in Bereketli. Our village was the scene of an on-going, and, particularly violent *kan davası* (blood feud), that periodically, throughout the past two decades, had erupted into violence. To date, in the years since it began, it had resulted in the violent deaths of no less than seven men, and the two extended families who were its chief protagonists each had several relatives serving time in the provincial prison in Balıkesir.

I do remember being taken by the *Muhtar* Kâmil to visit Balıkesir prison and meeting two different groups of Bereketlians who were housed there. It seems that they had learned of my presence in the village from relatives who had visited and expressed a desire to see for themselves who this American was. It may have been on that occasion that I heard the first details of the violence that smoldered just beneath the surface of our seemingly tranquil village life. I recall that, over time, I became aware not only of some of the vendetta's history, but also of the fact that the *Muhtar* was constantly aware that it could re-emerge at any moment. It was in anticipation of this possibility that he had been so insistent about no handguns being allowed at village weddings. I, subsequently, was to learn that part of the armed confrontation that had erupted at the village wedding had been a reaction to the possibility that the blood feud might erupt again, as the bride was related to one of the two warring families.

Gradually, I began to be able to tell some of the players in the conflict apart, largely due to the fact that they were always careful to avoid one another's company. Thus, if I happened to be sitting with a partisan of one side of the dispute and a member of the rival family, who just happened to be a close friend of mine, came into the coffee house, he would, despite my urgings, refuse to join our table and pointedly take a seat at the opposite end of the room. In retrospect, I think it was after one such occasion, when Ayhan Hangül (the man who had rejected my invitation to join us), recognizing that I had been hurt by his uncharacteristic action, provided me with some background on the *kan davası* as a way of explaining his behavior. Part of the problem was that in small villages such as ours, practically everyone was related in one way or another to one of the two warring parties.

I likewise do not recall when I became aware of the fact that one of the village elders, a man in his early seventies, who was called Hüseyin *Amca* (Uncle Hüseyin), was one of the principals in the dispute. His brother, some twenty years earlier, had been its first victim in a quarrel over ownership of a small plot of garden. I spent a good deal of time in the company of Uncle Hüseyin, as he was one of the men who frequented the village coffee house, and also he had taken it upon himself to assist me in learning proper Turkish (as he put it), rather than the profanity-ridden slang that served as the *lingua franca* in Bereketli.

Despite what I do not remember, there was one day when the blood feud forced its way into my life, a day that I will never be able to forget. It was a beautiful clear late Fall day and I was sitting with Hüseyin *Amca* sipping a cup of tea and smoking the proverbial hand-rolled cigarette. I remember watching as an elderly woman, accompanied by a younger woman and two small children, headed down the path across from the coffee house in the direction of the village vegetable gardens. They were just far enough away that I couldn't really make out their faces. A few moments later, Hüseyin *Amca* got up from the table, nodded a farewell, and left the coffee house in the direction earlier taken by the women and children.

Less than an hour had passed when the door to the coffee house opened and Hüseyin *Amca*, covered with blood, came through the door and sat down across from me in the same chair he had earlier vacated. Thinking he was hurt, I jumped up and asked if he needed help. He shook his head and turned to Şakir Durdu the *kahveci* and told him that he had better send word to the gendarmes in Konakpınar. From the stunned look on Şakir's face I realized that something bad must have happened.

I turned back to Hüseyin and asked again if there was anything I could do. He shook his head in the negative and said *"Niyahet bu iş bitti. O piç yuvasını temizledim. Koyunlar gibi hepsini boğazladım."* (Finally, this business is over. I cleaned up that nest of bastards. I slit all their throats like sheep.) I couldn't believe my ears, but as the coffee house began to fill, it became all too clear. Gentle Hüseyin *Amca* had left my side, followed the two women and two small children down to the village gardens, and cold-bloodedly slit their throats. As we waited for what seemed like an eternity for the gendarmes to arrive, he calmly described the reasoning behind his barbaric action.

He was an old man and his only surviving son was about to be released from prison (in the wake of the recent election a general amnesty of prisoners was anticipated) and return to the village where ten years earlier he had murdered two members of the rival family. All that was left of his enemy's immediate family were the mother, her daughter-in-law (both women had been widowed in earlier blood lettings) and the two small sons of one of the men Hüseyin *Amca*'s son was currently incarcerated for having killed.

As he related his story to the circle of stunned listeners, Hüseyin calmly sipped a glass of tea that Şakir had placed before him. He then continued to explain that he had nothing to fear himself, he was an old man and Turkish law prohibited the execution of anyone over sixty-five years of age. (A law that had recently spared the life of Celal Bayar, one of the co-founders of the *Demokrat Partisi* who had been President of the Republic when the 1960 coup occurred. It was his advanced age that kept him from swinging at the end of a rope next to Menderes.) Likewise the feud had taken what little resources the family may have once had and he had nothing to leave his son. "He had," he said, "thought long and hard about what he could do to ensure that his son did not have to live the rest of his life in the same fear and anticipation that he [Hüseyin], had lived his in." "I hadn't planned it," he said, "but when Hit and I were sitting here and I looked up and saw them all together, it came to me. Were I to get rid of all of them, I could guarantee that my son might be able to live in peace."

He knew that as long as the two boys of the man killed by his own son were alive, their mother and grandmother would be biding their time for the day that they grew old enough to be sent out to avenge their father's blood. Custom dictated that only sons had the unchallengeable duty to seek revenge against their father's killer and he was gambling that no less-closely related member of his enemy's clan would feel the need to go after his son for the events of that bloody November day in Bereketli.

In time, the gendarmes from Konakpınar arrived; we said our goodbyes and Hüseyin *Amca* was led away in chains. I never saw him again.

That night, as I related the tumultuous day's events to Jeannie, I remember that she listened to me with a growing look of horror on her face. When I finished, I asked her what the matter was, thinking that she had been really upset by what had happened. She looked at me and said "How could you relate this horrible story without any sign of emotion whatsoever?" I think it was at that point that I first became aware of the fact that perhaps I had been in Bereketli a bit too long. Life, death, and violence had become just another part of the day for me. Perhaps it was time to think about moving on.

Chapter 35

Yusuf *Amca*'s fire insurance policy

There was still one final act in the Bereketli *kan davası* (blood feud) saga that was to play itself out before I was to leave the village. A few weeks after the butchery perpetrated by Hüseyin *Amca*, I was awakened by loud voices outside my window. When I got up to see what was going on, I saw flames shooting out from a neighboring house. I quickly went outside to join a group of neighbors and we watched helplessly as the home of a partially paralyzed widower named Abdi *Dayı*, literally went up in flames.

Fortunately, he had gotten out of the house after the fire began and was now sitting on the ground quietly sobbing as he literally watched everything he owned in the world be consumed by fire. When I approached to offer my condolences I noticed the heavy stench of kerosene in the air and, after expressing my regrets with the formulaic *geçmiş olsun* (a catch-all phrase meaning 'May you recover soon, I'm sorry about your bad luck'), I moved over to a group of men who were standing nearby. I commented on the smell of kerosene in the air, and they knowingly nodded in agreement. Soon all that was left of Abdi *Dayı*'s house were the four stone walls. Gradually the onlookers began to disperse and I returned home to get a couple of hours sleep before my alarm clock (the *müezzin*'s call to morning prayers) went off.

When, a few hours later, I entered the village coffee house, there were a number of grave faces awaiting me and the conversation immediately turned to the previous night's tragedy. In the initial excitement the fact that Abdi *Dayı*'s house was located directly behind that of the now-imprisoned Hüseyin *Dayı* had escaped my notice, but the tone of the conversation made it clear that no one else had overlooked this coincidence. Someone who lived nearby mentioned hearing the sound of a jeep shortly before the fire began (an extremely rare occurrence at night in Bereketli) and another reported finding four empty bottles reeking of kerosene outside the charred remains of Abdi *Dayı*'s house.

As we continued our discussion it became clear that someone had hired a stranger (or strangers) to torch Hüseyin's house, and that on a moonless night, the arsonist had mistakenly set fire to the wrong residence. Once a consensus as to the likely cause of the arson had been agreed upon, talk turned to what a shame it was that one of the most harmless and truly gentle men in the village had been the victim of this cruel accident. After all the assembled had expressed their regrets that the innocent Abdi had been drawn into the *kan davası*, there was a moment of silence and then *Hırsız* Ibrahim turned to me and said "Hit, does this kind of thing happen in America?" By this time, my Turkish had improved to the point that I could fluently (if not always grammatically) respond to any and all queries and I explained that yes similar things could and did occur in my country as well.

The next question was "What happens in America when this kind of thing occurs?" I replied that most people had something called *yangın sigortası* (fire insurance) and that this provided them with the means to rebuild. After a lengthy description of the meaning and workings of insurance, all in attendance agreed that this was a useful concept and bemoaned the fact that there was nothing similar available in Bereketli.

As I listened to this discussion a thought came to me and I said "Of course, in rural America many people don't have fire insurance and in those communities they have another kind of insurance." Someone asked "What's that?" I continued, "The people who live in small villages like Bereketli serve as one another's insurance policies. If something like this happens to a neighbor, they come together and rebuild the house, knowing, that if it was their home that was destroyed, their neighbors would have done the same for them." I waited for a moment to let this sink in and then continued "Ali, you've got that *kireç* [lime used in mortar] in the shed next to your house, that you have no use for and, Ahmet you have that pile of *kereste* [lumber] in your yard left over from the house you built for your son last year." I next turned to Mustafa, and continued, "Didn't you tell me the other day that you had no use for those tiles from the roof of your father's old house that are stacked up in your yard?"

After close to two hours of discussion about whether or not this process could conceivably work in Bereketli, *Hırsız* Ibrahim (who was very poor, but a master carpenter) spoke up and said, "I don't have anything to give but my time, but if you are all willing to accept Hit's idea, I will work until the house is as good as new." Within moments, the *kahveci* Şakir was ordered to fetch some paper and a pen and a list of volunteers, together with what they could contribute, was quickly assembled.

Someone pointed out that the rebuilt house wouldn't be much use if there was nothing in it, and a second list was begun for items such as a mattress, a quilt, clothes (my landlord, the tailor Mehmet Sadık, pledged to make a new suit out of a piece of wool he had been saving – a useful gesture as Abdi *Dayı* had escaped with virtually nothing but the night shirt on his back), cooking pots, a plate, a spoon, etc.

There was a sense of communal excitement in the air that was like nothing I had previously experienced in Bereketli. A short time later we adjourned and everyone returned home to collect what they had pledged as their contribution to Abdi *Dayı*'s 'fire insurance.' Before leaving, we agreed to meet bright and early the next morning. I had suggested we do so immediately – afraid that the enthusiasm might dissipate during the night – but someone pointed out that the embers were still hot and we agreed to begin work at 6 a.m. the following day.

I went off with Ahmet (the owner of the unused lumber), to help carry the *kereste* he had agreed to donate to the construction site. While we were doing so, several other men joined us. The owner of one of the two tractors in the village took a couple of the older boys with him and set off with his *römork* (open trailer) to bring a load of sand from the river for the mortar we would need. By nightfall, the area around Abdi's house had indeed begun to look like a construction site and I went to bed assured that we really were going to be able to make a bit of a difference.

The *Muhtar* had gone with Abdi *Dayı* to the *Nahiye* center in Konakpınar early that morning, to report the arson and fill out the endless forms that accompanied such incidents, and when he returned he was delighted (and somewhat surprised) to see what had been accomplished in his absence. He quickly embraced the project and thereafter loved to tell the story of how Hit *Bey* had managed to do something that had never occurred in the one hundred and fifty year history of the village, namely, inspire people to voluntarily participate in a community project, rather than in response to the labor *corvée* known as *imece* (in 1965 the head of each village household owed three days a year of labor on community projects determined by the *Muhtar*).

It was less my inspiring speech than it was the fact that when someone so vulnerable and obviously the victim of extremely bad luck (first his stroke that led to the paralysis, then the untimely death of his wife, and now the fire) is in danger, it is easy to assist. The *Muhtar* was right on one point however, Bereketlians came together as never before to right what was so obviously a wrong.

We were lucky, the weather, while cold, stayed nice, and within two weeks we had virtually rebuilt Abdi *Dayı*'s house. Midway through the third week he was back in his own home, dressed in the new suit that had been Mehmet Sadık's contribution to the communal effort.

Chapter 36

Karabaş eats too much bread

At some point midway through my stay in Bereketli I had befriended and then unconsciously adopted a stray *Sivas kangal* (sheep dog from Sivas in Central Anatolia). I say adopted, but in fact he already had an owner. The problem was, that as his owner no longer had a flock of sheep, he had no use for the dog (whom I named *Karabaş*) and therefore saw little to be gained by feeding him. *Karabaş* was a prime specimen of this breed of fierce sheep dogs and he wore the typical spiked collar to keep his throat protected against his natural enemy, the wolf. He also had the scars to prove that he knew what his role in life was all about.

I had encountered my first *Kangal* on my very first excursion out of the village, the day we had been searching for a lost sheep and ended up in the *Alevi* village of Kuşkaya. My first impression was not that positive as I had wandered off from the group and stumbled into a shepherd and his flock from a neighboring village. His *Kangal* took a justifiable objection to my presence and looked as if he was about to eat me for a late lunch. As I debated whether it was better to try and run or just stand still and be eaten, one of my companions ran up. Seeing what was going on, he simply leaned down as if to pick up a rock, and the *Kangal*, that a moment earlier had been considering which part of me he wanted to devour first, put his tail between his legs and went running off. My friend explained that this was the proper routine for dealing with this type of dog and assured me that it always worked. I later realized that it was the fact that people (village children in particular) who were always throwing stones at them, that had taught the *Kangal*s to flee at the sight of a human being bending down. Turkish villagers really do not like dogs, although in recognition of their role in protecting an important part of their livelihood, their flocks, they do tolerate the *Kangal*.

Karabaş, meaning 'Black Head,' was a giant specimen of a breed known for its size. He weighed close to a hundred pounds and stood as tall as my waist. In addition, he possessed an enormous head and it was truly black. I would not say that we ever really became friends, but I fed him, and he, in acknowledgement of my role as sustenance provider, tolerated me. He didn't particularly like to be petted, but he was a ferocious watch dog, a fact that made him acceptable to my second landlord, Mehmet Sadık. He had not been so popular when I was living in the mosque courtyard, as he seemed to be a true secularist, and on occasion, had taken exception to the worshippers arriving for prayers in what he considered to be his front yard.

When I moved to Mehmet Sadık's house, he grew even larger, as a good portion of Cini's attempts at baking over a single gas burner with a little tin oven perched over its flame, seemed to end up in his stomach. The villagers soon realized that American women did not know how to bake bread and thereafter we were the recipients every week of much more bread than we could possibly have eaten in a month. *Karabaş*, however, had an insatiable appetite and not wishing to show disrespect to the staff of life by throwing out such gifts, a good portion of the largesse we were the beneficiaries of ended up in his stomach.

Life for *Karabaş* seemed good, until the day there was a pounding at my door and when I opened it I found a very distraught friend with a shotgun in his hand. "Hit *Bey*," he said, "come quickly, *Karabaş* has gone mad and, as he is your dog, no one else will shoot him." I quickly grabbed my coat and we went running out onto the road. I had no trouble following the trail left by *Karabaş*, as he had left a tornado-like path of destruction in his wake. There were ducks and chickens on rooftops and in trees, there was a donkey crippled by a vicious bite to his withers, and, as we approached the coffee house there was a dead lamb that had practically been decapitated. Near the school house we came upon a group of villagers who had cornered a panting, sweat-lathered, *Karabaş* between a wall and the corner of a house. Held at bay by rakes and shovels he, with his massive teeth barred, was simply waiting, as if for my arrival.

There were several guns present and I asked a close friend to do the necessary deed, as I simply didn't have the heart to do it myself. He acquiesced to my suggestion and, as I turned my head, I heard two shots. A shovel was procured and with help from several others we dug a hole in a corner of the schoolyard and buried *Karabaş*. I spent the rest of the afternoon trying to determine (and pay for) the damage he had done.

As evening approached I entered the village coffee house to find that the saga of mad *Karabaş* was the major topic of discussion. I quickly learned that a consensus had been reached prior to my arrival as to the cause for his bizarre behavior and that one and all were in agreement: I was the cause of his lunatic rampage through the streets of Bereketli. The problem, I was informed, was that I had given him too much food, and, in particular, too much bread. You simply can't feed a *Kangal* on a regular basis, I was told, as this is something they are not used to. Failure to observe this simple rule, I was informed, results in what we had experienced that day.

Now that the *Kangal* has become a recognized and, indeed, highly prized, breed in Europe and in the US in particular, I wonder if those individuals who pay up to $3000 for a purebred specimen are informed that if they overfeed their new pet he is liable to cut a swath of death across their neighborhood.

Chapter 37

Şoför Niyazi's revenge: the Peace Corps visits Bereketli in my absence

What were to be my last few months in Bereketli were marred by the fact that my wife Jeanne fell victim to a particular nasty case of hepatitis. This necessitated her hospitalization in Izmir and meant that I spent close to two months shuttling back and forth between the village and the American Military Hospital in that city.

During one of my absences from Bereketli, absences that not only were known to, but approved by the Peace Corps Headquarters in Ankara, a Peace Corps-CARE staffer named Walter Salmon decided to pay an unscheduled visit to the village. He happened to do so on a day when the *Muhtar* was in Balıkesir, that also coincidentally was a day that *Şoför* Niyazi's bus was inoperative.

In the months since his disruption of the wedding and subsequent flight from the village, Niyazi had managed to work out a fragile *modus vivendi* or truce with the *Muhtar* and, reportedly having promised to give up his gun-totting habits, had been allowed to return to the village, where he had resumed his role as owner-operator of one of our two links to the outside world.

When Salmon's jeep pulled up in front of the village coffee house, he was greeted by *Şoför* Niyazi, who was engaged in patching up his *otobüs,* in hopes of not missing the next day's run to the capital too. Niyazi, whose dislike for me was overshadowed only by his hatred of the *Muhtar*, never missed an opportunity to step into the role of his political nemesis and that day was no exception. He jumped at the chance to play host and ushered Salmon and a companion into the coffee house, where for the next two hours, in answer to their queries about my activities, he regaled them with tales of how my presence in the village had been a disruptive one and told them that the sooner I was removed the happier the residents of Bereketli would be.

This particular staffer and I had a bit of history between us, as he had been one of the 'experts' who had participated in our initial training program prior to our departure for Turkey. His expertise ostensibly stemmed from the fact that as a member of the very first Peace Corps group to serve in Turkey, he had 'visited a number of villages,' and was therefore brought back to the US to share his insights with our group of trainees.

During the two weeks he spent with us he was continuously barraged with questions about why we had not been provided with so much as a single book about Turkish village life. In answer to all such queries, he replied that there simply was no such literature available. He happened to be sharing a room with me and several other trainees, and, the day before his scheduled departure, I took advantage of a break in the program and went back to the room to pick up something. I was surprised to see arrayed on his bed, an open suitcase (that he was in the process of packing), together with a handful of books dealing with life in Turkish villages, the very works that he had been telling us for two weeks didn't exist. I jotted down their titles and, when later in the day we sat down with Salmon for what was to be our last session, enquired yet once again about why we had not been provided any reading materials. When he repeated the by-then familiar litany about the absence of such works, I said "That's strange, then how do you account for the fact that earlier today the following books were lying on your bed next to your open suitcase?" I then proceeded to read off the list of titles I had written down to the assembled body.

This led to a near mutiny among my fellow trainees, all of whom shared with me an almost pathological need to absorb anything and everything with any possible relevance to the undertaking we were about to begin. We suspected that Salmon (who in reality knew virtually nothing about Turkish village life), had been reading these works to garner information before each of the sessions he held with us. His unwillingness to share them stemmed from the fact that had he done so, it would have become apparent to all of us that he was simply regurgitating what he had been reading.

Salmon hemmed and hawed in response to the increasingly heated questions regarding his lack of candor, and finally his boss, a man named Chuck Lasky, the CARE official who was actually to administer our program, was forced to step in and admit that there had been some trouble getting copies for us of the books in question and therefore they had decided that Walter should simply share their contents with us. This didn't sit well with the group, most of whom were recent university graduates and quite capable of reading for themselves, and both Lasky and Salmon's credibility dropped a notch as a result of my exposure of their ineptitude.

As time would prove, both of these men were not only inept but petty, and I was soon to learn that they would not forget the loss of face they had suffered due to my inquisitiveness. Two weeks later, as the training portion of our program was winding up, I was called into the office of a woman named Barbara Dirks (an official of the Putney, Vermont based 'Experiment in International Living,' the group the Peace Corps had contracted our training out to), who had the overall responsibility for our three-month program in Turkish Language and Area Studies. She was a woman with a great deal of experience in running international programs and we had developed a good relationship. She confided in me the fact that both Salmon and Lasky had insistently demanded that I be dropped from the program and not be sent to Turkey. However, she continued, as, in her view and that of the remainder of the staff, I was one of the more promising of the trainees, she had vetoed their objections (something she had never done before), and due to her intervention on my behalf I was to be included in the group destined for Turkey. She warned me however of the need to be extremely careful in my dealing with these two men and to give neither of them anything that could be used against me in the future.

This was the same Walter Salmon, who, in my absence, just happened to stop by Bereketli on, what in Peace Corps jargon was known as, a 'site visit,' the purpose of which was to visit the volunteers and see if they had any needs he could help address (in this instance there was no volunteer in the village, a fact that Salmon was well aware of). As Niyazi spun out his tales of my unpopularity and misdoings, Salmon (as we were later to learn from others who were in the coffee house during their exchange) wrote furiously and frequently asked the type of pointed questions that made it clear that he was interested in any dirt that his interlocutor could provide, thereby increasing *Şoför* Niyazi's confidence, so that with each additional tall tale the tone of his comments became ever more critical. Two kindred spirits had met and they had a common dislike: the absent me.

When the *Muhtar* returned from the capital Salmon and his companion were long gone, but those who had overheard his exchanges with *Şoför* Niyazi lost no time in filling him in with the details of what had transpired in his absence. Unbeknownst to me, that evening a second extraordinary meeting of the heads of Bereketli's one hundred and twenty-eight households was convened. Once again, I was the subject, but now the issue was not how I was to be fed (as it had been on the night of my arrival seventeen months earlier), but rather what could be done to undo the damage caused by Niyazi's petty revenge. It was decided that the best course of action would be for the *Muhtar* to write a letter to the Peace Corps Director in Ankara, in an effort to set the record straight as to what I had been doing in the previous seventeen months, and, most importantly, to convey how the villagers actually felt about me. I was later to learn that this meeting lasted close to three hours, and, after the *Muhtar* had drafted the proposed letter, once again (as they had on my first night in the village) one hundred and twenty-eight men lined up to sign the missive. This letter, a copy and translation of which are appended to this book, has followed me round the world in the past four decades and, when I dug it out of my papers a few months ago and reread it, I was immediately transported back in time to the days when I was part of the village of Bereketli. It was, in fact, the rereading of that letter and the memories it evoked, that finally prompted me to sit down and begin writing the present account.

When, a few days after this incident, I returned from Izmir to Bereketli, I was greeted by the *Muhtar*, who enquired as to whether I had heard anything from Ankara. I sensed that there was something he wanted to tell me and without much urging he related the above events. The letter had already been dispatched, but he shared with me the tone of its contents in the form of two early drafts that he had saved and I began to get a sense of just how much the visit of Walter Salmon and its aftermath had upset the equilibrium of village life. I don't recall being particularly upset in a personal sense, as I had long been accustomed to the ineptitude of the Ankara Peace Corps-CARE staff, but I was livid about the fact that Salmon's visit had clearly caused unnecessary concern to my friends and hosts. I assured the *Muhtar* that there was nothing to worry about and, for my own part, resolved to get to the bottom of this matter at the earliest opportunity.

The chance to do so came quicker than I had anticipated as, a few days later, I received a telegram from Ankara informing me that together with the other members of my group I was being summoned to a meeting the following week. Armed with the drafts of the village letter I set off for the capital. On the long train ride between Balıkesir and Ankara I had plenty of time to think and had decided that rather than discuss the matter with Lasky (who was most likely behind the visit in the first place), I would go straight to the overall director of the Peace Corps in Turkey. Accordingly, upon my arrival in Ankara, I marched into the office of the new Director, Dr David Berlew, a former MIT Professor of Psychology, who was as distinguished as his predecessor Prichard had been undistinguished.

Berlew had let it be known that he intended to have an open-door policy when it came to volunteers wishing to speak to him. True to his word, he told the secretary to send me in. After I explained the purpose of my visit, he quickly asked his secretary to clear his calendar, and I spent the next two hours briefing him on both my own concerns and the problems in our group that had resulted from Peace Corps having contracted out the running of our program to CARE International. I held back nothing of the frustration that had been building virtually since the training program and, at Berlew's insistence, translated and read him the draft of the letter that I had been given by the *Muhtar* in Bereketli.

At one point, Berlew picked up the telephone and called Chuck Lasky (whose office was downstairs) and, without giving him a reason, requested that he immediately send up the actual letter addressed to the Peace Corps Director (who was after all Berlew not Lasky), that had been sent by the *Muhtar* of Bereketli regarding the activities of a volunteer named Heath Lowry. From the one side of the conversation I was privy to it quickly became apparent that Lasky was claiming that there was no such letter, but when pressed admitted that maybe something of that nature had arrived, but that there hadn't been time for it to be translated. Berlew told him in no uncertain terms that he wanted the letter immediately and hung up. A couple of minutes later, Lasky himself appeared and, unable to disguise his shock at seeing me, handed over the requested document.

Berlew asked him to sit down and handed me the letter, saying that as Lasky had not had time to have it translated, maybe I would be kind enough to do so for them. I did what he requested and then listened as Berlew queried Lasky as to whether its contents jibbed with the report he had received from his staffer following the unscheduled visit to Bereketli. Lasky, to his credit, did not try to hide the fact that what he had just heard bore no relationship to the report submitted by Salmon, and Berlew asked him to bring a copy of the 'site visit' report.

A few minutes later Lasky re-entered the room and handed Berlew a copy of the Salmon site visit report. After quickly perusing it, he turned to Lasky and said, "Where are the signatures?" Lasky seemed stunned and said "What do you mean?" Berlew replied that the letter I had translated for them, while written by the *Muhtar*, had been signed by one hundred and twenty-eight men of the village, a fact that clearly was news to Lasky. He then pointed out that the Salmon report not only lacked the authentication of the villagers he claimed sought my removal, it did not even name them. He then looked at Lasky and said "I don't think we really want this report in Heath's file, do we?" When Lasky nodded his agreement, he tore the paper in half and dropped it in his wastepaper basket. Lasky, sensing that the meeting was over, got up to leave and I followed suit.

Before leaving, I turned to Berlew and asked him if he had any objection to my keeping the original of the *Muhtar*'s letter and the signatures appended to it, as it clearly was of more importance to me than it was to the CARE-Peace Corps office staff, who after all hadn't even bothered to read it. He smiled, removed the letter from the file, and handed it to me. Thus ended the most satisfying encounter I ever had with a representative of the Peace Corps Staff in Turkey.

My meeting with Berlew was to have another benefit, as when a few months later I found myself back in Washington, D.C., in need of a job it was a call from him to his brother Kingston (the number three man in Peace Corps Washington), that resulted in me being hired to recruit for the Peace Corps.

Chapter 38

Leaving Bereketli:
'Hit, don't forget, you are now one of us.
There are things you have seen and heard
here in Bereketli that no one else
need know about'

At the beginning of February 1966 the Peace Corps doctors determined that, weakened as she was by her prolonged bout with hepatitis, Jeanne could not return to village life, and she was flown back to Washington, D.C., for additional treatment. The initial word I received was that I was to continue working in Bereketli until the end of my scheduled term, that was set for early June. When I protested at what seemed like yet another arbitrary and insensitive staff decision, I was told that I was welcome to leave, but doing so would mean that I paid my return airfare out of my own pocket. This was out of the question, for while I had survived nicely on my 327 TL ($36.50) monthly salary, I had not put aside anything resembling the sum needed for a plane ticket. Indeed, in the previous two months, my frequent running back and forth between Bereketli and Izmir had virtually bankrupted me.

Therefore, after putting Jeanne on the plane, I returned to Bereketli for what, unbeknownst to me, was to be my last month in

The village gathers for the Children's Holiday (23 April)

the village (when Jeanne arrived in Washington, for additional medical treatment, her doctors quickly determined that it would be in her best interest were I to return as well – but as yet I was unaware of this new development). Now, I had yet another new status: in eighteen months I had gone from bachelor, to married man, and now to married man living alone. Now, just as had been the case upon my arrival, I found myself invited into the homes of what were now old friends for dinner every day.

A couple of weeks later, I received a telegram from Ankara informing me that Peace Corps Washington had decided that I was to return to the US, and that I should be ready to do so by the end of the month. The first person I shared this news with was my friend, the *Muhtar* Kâmil. During the next couple of days, as I began to pack up what few belongings I would take with me, he never left my side and we spent numerous hours reminiscing over the events of the past months.

A constant *leitmotif* in our conversations, stated in various fashions, was 'Hit, don't forget, you are now one of us. There are things that you have seen and heard in Bereketli that no one else need know about.' To understand the sentiment underlying that admonition one has only to compare the accounts of various events as I have related them in the preceding pages, with the version of the same events as recounted in the *Muhtar*'s letter to the Peace Corps Director. A few examples will serve to illustrate this point.

While, in his letter the *Muhtar* proudly related my role in the tragic poisoning of the young mother, Emine, he made it sound as if her taking of the *kekik yağı* (oil of thyme) was a simple accident, rather than the result of the terrible ignorance concerning all matters concerning health that was the norm in Bereketli:

> "It was in those days that a case of poisoning, that was related to a birth, occurred. A member of Mehmed Sadık Özkan's family was poisoned as a result of drinking some oil of thyme. Despite the fact that the village was filled with their relatives, it was Hit, who having taken off his own overcoat and wrapped her in it, on a very cold night, with absolutely no regard for his own health, took her to a doctor in Balıkesir in an open wagon pulled by a tractor. Believe me, this action brought tears to the eyes of the villagers."

To have told the story as it actually occurred, would have (in his mind) negatively reflected upon his fellow villagers, whom he had often bemoaned to me were *kara cahil* (grossly ignorant). While such talk was alright among friends, this certainly was not an image to be shared with strangers. More tellingly, in an effort not to deflect from his desire to show me in the best light possible, he neglected to mention the ending of the oil of thyme story. Regardless of whatever efforts I had taken, the truth of the matter was that at the end of the day Emine had died. This rather important fact did not find its way into his account.

In his recounting of the planting of the poplar trees, while once again, stressing my role in getting them into the ground, he skims over the fact that at the urging of *Şoför* Niyazi (who remains unnamed throughout his narrative), there was initially a reluctance on the part of the villagers to participate in the planting. This fact is only hinted at in his letter:

"One day he explained the advantages of planting poplar trees. And we, taking up his suggestion, planted 400 poplar tree seedlings next to the road leading to Balıkesir. At that time we had a religious preacher in the village.... Our *Hoca* (Preacher), who was fond of repeating that from a religious perspective the planting and nurturing of a tree was a most meritorious, indeed praiseworthy, act managed to conveniently disappear and did not participate in the planting of the trees. Hit, on the other hand, planted a minimum of thirty trees. And I held Hit up as an example to the villagers. This is our country, if an American can expend effort in all ways on its behalf, why is it that we don't do the same?"

Aside from his oblique reference to having held my actions up as an example to the villagers and in his criticism of the *Hoca*'s failure to participate in the communal exercise, there is no hint at all of Niyazi's role in trying to undermine the poplar tree planting project. To have done otherwise, would have meant airing the village's dirty laundry in public.

Finally, in his version of the incident of the rebuilding of the house destroyed by the arsonist's torch, he wrote:

"Most recently, there was an incident of a fire in the village. An elderly paralyzed man's house was burnt in an act of arson. To rebuild that house, Hit worked for days like a common laborer."

In this case, while surprisingly he does not hide the fact that the house was destroyed due to arson (*evi kundaklanmak suretile yakıldı*), he makes no mention of the bitter blood feud and the gruesome murders, that precipitated it. To do so, would once again, have cast the village (both he and I so loved) into a less-than-positive light.

Indeed, far more telling than the incidents he chose to recall, are the all-important ones he chose to overlook. Thus, the blood feud (*kan davası*), the gunfire at the village wedding and the ensuing night of terror, and the ongoing struggle of wills between the *Muhtar* and me on one side, and *Şoför* Niyazi on the other, is passed over in silence.

Even in his letter, while having felt that some explanation for what prompted its writing was called for, he never even hints at the disruptive role played by *Şoför* Niyazi in lying to the gullible Walter Salmon. Rather, he suggests that he thinks there may have been some unspecified misunderstanding that occurred in the course of Salmon's visit:

"Not long ago, an assistant director, accompanied by another person, came to the village. In my opinion, his poor grasp of Turkish was the cause of his misunderstanding of what has transpired. This has distressed the entire village. As a village we are all very satisfied with Hit. The purpose of this letter, written with the deepest of sincerity, is to communicate to you our distress over this misunderstanding."

He, while fully aware that his missive was written in direct response to the misinformation communicated by our friend Niyazi, chose to credit it to Salmon's "poor grasp of Turkish" (in fact it was not this staffer's Turkish – that was good – but his judgment that was questionable), thereby once again managing to conceal the fact that there was even so much as a single dissenting opinion in the village as to the effectiveness of my role.

By the same token, Kâmil downplayed his own role in facilitating the manner in which he had helped make me not only acceptable to but well liked by the villagers. Here, one has only to recall that extraordinary meeting he convened, on the night of my arrival, where he convinced the villagers to host and feed me in their homes. It was that single act that was to make my experience in Bereketli truly unique. No other member of our group was to be provided such an *entrée* into their new lives, and what little I was able to accomplish, all directly stemmed from the opportunity I was thus afforded to literally meet (and be met by) each and every member of the village in the course of my first four months in Bereketli. This too he neglected to mention, as to have done so would have made it appear that he was trumpeting his own role as host.

Thus, when Kâmil, as my departure neared, reminded me on more than one occasion 'Hit, don't forget, you are now one of us. There are things that you have seen and heard here in Bereketli that no one else need know about,' there was no doubt in my mind as to what he was referring. The silence I have maintained in the past forty-three years stems primarily from his request. If I have chosen to break that trust in setting down this account it is due to several facts. First, and foremost, is the sad reality that only a very small handful of the one hundred and twenty-eight men who opened their doors and hearts to me in Bereketli are still alive today. Kâmil, *nur içinde yatsın* (may he rest in peace), himself has been dead for twenty years. Second, is a growing awareness of my own mortality, an awareness heightened by a recent bout with cancer of the throat. (Perhaps brought on by all those hand-rolled, home-grown tobacco cigarettes I smoked in Bereketli. Or maybe, it was the newspaper print that served as their wrappings?) This awareness, coupled with a feeling that the many acts of friendship and kindness I experienced as a temporary citizen of Bereketli deserve to be known by a wider audience, are what has led to my decision to set down on paper this account of my formative eighteen-month sojourn in Bereketli. In all the years that have passed since I left my village home, it has never been far from my thoughts. I realized just how true that statement really is when I sat down to write about my village life and the words just seemed to find their own way onto the paper.

If, in so doing, I am breaking that trust implicit in the *Muhtar* Kâmil's injunction, I do so in the hope that he and today's Bereketlians will comprehend my motives. To say that my time in the village was filled with blessedness (*bereketli*), would be an understatement. I truly came of age in Bereketli.

Appendix

The *Muhtar* Kâmil's letter to the Director of the Peace Corps

January 30, 1966
Bereketli Village

To the Director of the Peace Corps
Ankara

I, Kâmil Aslantekin, am the *Muhtar* (elected representative) of the village of Bereketli, that is located in the *Nahiye* (County) of Konakpınar, 25 kilometers from the provincial capital Balıkesir. Following the Revolution, with the support of 100% of my fellow villagers, I replaced the village school teacher as *Muhtar*. At the urging of my people, I entered the recent elections and was elected *Muhtar* with 80% of the vote. When it comes to personal benefit, the position of *Muhtar* in Turkey does not even cover 3% of a family's expenses. The post of *Muhtar* can only be accepted as a public service. As the son of a backward nation, while faced with these types of state problems, we were aware of the fact that, out of its generosity, the American government, in the name of its people, provided assistance [to other nations]. But we could never have dreamed that the Americans could be so humble, respectful and, at the same time, such a selfless people. We learned this was in fact the case from the actions of Hit [Heath] – and as a village we responded with appreciation to the goodness of the American nation – it was at the time that Hit and Bani [Bonnie] had first come to our village. As we are all aware they didn't really know Turkish. It was in those days that a case of poisoning, that was related to a birth, occurred. A member of Mehmed Sadık Özkan's family was poisoned as a result of drinking some oil of thyme. Despite the fact that the village was filled with their relatives, it was Hit, who having taken off his own over-coat and wrapped her in it, on a very cold night, with absolutely no regard for his own health, took her to a doctor in Balıkesir in an open wagon pulled by a tractor. Believe me, this action brought tears to the eyes of the villagers. In the village, whenever someone was in need of treatment for any kind of cuts or bruises, he would humbly go to their houses and treat them. In my opinion I have written enough about matters of health. At this time, Hit was residing in the village meeting room and we frequently had the opportunity to benefit from his suggestions and ideas. One day he explained the advantages of planting poplar trees. And we, taking up his suggestion, planted 400 poplar tree seedlings next to the road leading to Balıkesir. At that time we had a religious preacher in the village. He liked to talk about the 20th century. Our *Hoca* (Preacher), who was fond of repeating that from a religious perspective the planting and nurturing of a tree was a most meritorious, indeed praiseworthy act, managed to con-veniently disappear and did not participate in the planting of the trees. Hit, on the other hand, planted a minimum of thirty trees. And I held Hit up as an example to the villagers. This is our country, if an American can expend effort in all ways on its behalf, why is it that we don't do the same? In the village it was customary to wash vegetables and laundry in the foun-tains. It was in response to a suggestion of his that we banned this prac-tice. Likewise, across from the village school we built a model house. In this project Hit played a large role. Again, he was responsible for building a water depot next to the village coffee house. As a result, Hit's actions served as a model, where previously it was only possible to complete a vil-lage project with the use of *imece* [Note: a corvée, under which villagers were forced to annually provide a set number of days of free labor for the good of the community]. We went to assist the Konakpınar County Administrative Head with the building of a bridge in the village of Kumlugedik [*sic.* Kumgedik]. There, Hit worked harder than anyone. Seeing this brought tears to the eyes of the *Nahiye* Administrator. There were so many things [he did] that words don't suffice to explain them all. Most recently, there was an incident of a fire in the village. An elderly par-alyzed man's house was burnt in an act of arson. To rebuild that house, Hit worked for days like a common laborer. Our village has a one hundred and fifty year history. If one weighs what has been accomplished in the past years, against all that was done in the previous one hundred and fifty years, believe me more has been done in the past three years. So far three new houses have been built using the example of our model house. This is the single greatest advantage to the village. If we think upon this house, it becomes obvious that from the perspective of enriching our national wealth, in my opinion it is a most important step. It is sixteen months since Hit arrived in our village. During this time, when we had a visit from the Director of the Peace Corps, we told him all these things with pride. Not long ago, an assistant director, accompanied by another person, came to the village. In my opinion, his poor grasp of Turkish was the cause of his misunderstanding of what has transpired. This has distressed the entire village. As a village we are all very satisfied with Hit. The purpose of this letter, written with the deepest of sincerity, is to communicate to you our distress over this misunderstanding. Please accept this with the most sincere respect and appreciation of my village.

The *Muhtar* (Elected Head) of the Village of Bereketli
KÂMİL ASLANTEKİN

1) Nazım Çakan
2) Muhterem Dilmaç
3) M. Sadık Dilek
4) Kerametin Dilek
5) Ayhan Hangül
6) M. Sadık Demirel
7) İbrahim Dilek
8) Mehmet Savaş
9) Recep Berghan
10) M. Ali Kaygı
11) Necdet Can
12) İlhami Duman
13) Niyazi Koç
14) Halil Ergün
15) Celil İlhan
16) Sadetdin Cengiz
17) İbrahim Esender
18) Fikret Yılmaz
19) Baki Yılmaz
20) Necip Can
21) Hakkı Balcan
22) Sabri Yılmaz
23) Adil Balgün

24) Özcan Çakan
25) Halıtdın Cengiz
26) Memet Demiralp
27) Vesat Hazanap
28) Ahmet Alp
29) Şaban Özdemir
30) Hüseyin Balcan
31) İlhan Vedat
32) Nazım Gültekin
33) Adem Demiralp
34) Süleyman Dağdelen
35) Amet İlhan
36) Feyzi Dursun
37) İbrahim Kandemir
38) Hasan Dilmaç
39) İsak Cengiz
40) Sadatdin Ata
41) Naci Er
42) Bayram Ata
43) Orhan Demiralp
44) İdris Kayahan
45) Hakkı İlhan

46) Orhan Yılmaz
47) Sami Dilek
48) Mehmet Demiralp
49) M. Sadık Çakmak
50) İbrahim Gelenbevi
51) Buran Can
52) Erdoğan Can
53) İdris Dilek
54) M. Ali Ersoy
55) Cahit Cengiz
56) Şayir Aplay
57) Yusuf İlhan
58) Halil Alp
59) Recep Dağdelen
60) Süleyman Çakır
61) Selatdin Dilmaç
62) Süleyman Aplay
63) M. Sadık Gözhan
64) Kemal İlhan
65) Mehmet Karaaslan
66) Ahmet Bozanalp
67) Halil Çetin

68) Idris İlhan
69) Hilmi Konmaz
70) M. Ali Balgün
71) Servet Dogankan
72) Eyüp Bayat
73) Ismail Alınmış
74) Ismail Baltaş
75) Riza Demiralp
76) Idris Kaydemir
77) Şakir Durdu
78) Ibrahim Dolu
79) Mustafa Gezer
80) Recep Balgün
81) H. Huseyin Dilek
82) Ismail Balgün
83) Hüseyin Karaman
84) Abil Balgül
85) Turan Alp
86) Turhan İrkil
87) Ahmet Duman
88) Avni Erdem
89) Ali Dilmaç

90) Ismail Kayğı
91) Ilhami Er
92) Davut İlhan
93) Ibrahim Koç
94) Hasan Özdemir
95) Ersin Demirel
96) Ünal Ilhan
97) Irfan Dilmaç
98) Sezai Duman
99) M. Sadık
      Doğantekin
100) Yüksel Koç
101) Enver Erdoğan
102) Hayri Aslantekin
103) Hasan Bayat
104) Tahsin Demirtaş
105) Mustafa Koç
106) Ibrahim Ata
107) Bedritdin Can
108) Özet Doğantekin
109) Arif Aslantekin
110) Vahit Erdoğan

111) Rifat Demirel
112) Musa Er
113) Ali Gezer
114) Kamil Bolak
115) Ümmet
      Doğantekin
116) Ismail Can
117) Emin Demirkol
118) Hüseyin Bozanalp
119) Haram Hüseyin
120) Bediritdin Cengiz
121) Muamber Erdem
122) Ceaml Dilek
123) Mehmet Balcan
124) Kamil Doğantekin
125) Mehmet Can
126) Mustafa
      Doğantekin
127) Sedat Demirel
128) Halit Çakan

I certify that the above-listed names and signatures are those of heads of the families in our village, and that the signatures are their own.

Transcription of Kamil Aslantekin's Turkish Handwritten Letter to Ankara

30-1-1966
Bereketli Köyü

Barıs Gönüllüleri Müdürlüğüne
Ankara

Ben Balıkesir Vilayetine (25) kilometre mesafede Konakpınar Nahiyesinin Bereketli Köyü Muhtarı Kâmil Aslantekinim. İnkilâpta, öğretmenden Muhtarlık vazifesini köyümün yüzde yüz isteğiyle Muhtar oldum. Ve yine seçime istirak, halkın isteğiyle girib, yüzde (80) farkla Muhtar seçildim. Türkiyede Muhtarlık vazifesi menfaat yönünden bir ailenin (100) de üç ihtiyacı sağlanmaz. Yalnız Muhtarlık vazifesi amme işi olarak, kabul edilir. Bu gibi Memleket davalarını düşünerek geri kalmış bir Memleketin öz evlâdı olarak, köyümün maddi ve manevi ihtiyaçları içinde çırpınırken, Amerikan Devletini'nin nimetlerinden, devlet namı altında yardımlar yapıldığını biliyorduk. Fakat Amerikalıların bukadar mütevazi ve hürmetgâr, aynı zaman da bilursiz bir insan oldukları aklın bile kabul edeceği bir iş değildi. İste bu yazdığım misallerin hakikat olduğunu hit (Heath)in hareketleri ile anladık -- ve köylülerimiz arasında bir Amerikan milletinin nekadar iyi bir millet olduğu taktirle karşılandı – işte bu aralarda Hit (Heath) ve Bani (Bonnie) yeni köyümüze gelmiş idi. Yalnız hepimizin malûmu Türkçe bilmiyorlardı. Bu arada köyde bir doğum yüzünden zehirlenme vakası oldu. Mehmed Sadık Özkanın ailesi kekik yağı içmek suretile zehirlenmiş idi. Köyde bütün akrabası olduğu halde açık arabalı bir tıraktörle Hitin sırtından çıkardığı palto ile örtünmek süretile o soğuk havada hiç kendi sıhatini düşünmeden Balıkesire doktora götürdü. Bu hareketi Türk köylüsünü inanın ağlattı. Köyde kimde bir tedavi edilecek yara kesik olursa olsun gönülsüz hastaların evine gidip onları tedavi etti. Sağlık yönün den bu kadar yazdığım bence kafi. Hit bu aralarda köy heyet odasında duruyordu biz de onun fikirlerinden istifade ediyorduk. Birgün kavak ekme mevzuunu bize anlattı. Ve biz de onun fikirinden istifade etmek suretile Balıkesir yolu üzerine (400) adet yeni tip kavak ektik. Bu arada Köyümüzde Vaiz Hocamız vardı. Yirminci asırdan bas ediyordu. Dini yönden bir fidan yetiştirmek çok sevap olduğunu söyleyen Hocalarımız tenezül edip kavak ekmeğe gelmediler. Hit enaz otuz kavak ekti. Ve missal olarak Hiti köylülere gösterdim. Bu memleket, bizim bir Amerikalı her yönden çaba gösteriyorda, bizler neden calışmıyoruz dedim. Çeşmelerde sebze ve bez yıkanıyordu. Bunu da onun fikri ile yasak ettik. Ayrıca köye, örnek, bir okulumuz önüne ev yaptık onun yapılmasında Hitin çok rölü oldu. Ayrıca köy kahvesinin yanına bir havuz yapıldı. Netice imece suretile yapılan her köy işinde de Hit örnek misaller Verdi. Konakpınar Nahiye Müdürü ile Kumlugedik köyüne köprü yardımına gittik. Orada Hit en yüksek yardımda bulundu. Bu hal Nahiye Müdürünü ağlattı. Netice itibariyle anlatmakla tükenmez. Son olarak köyümüzde bir yangın hadisesi oldu. Felçli bir şahsinn evi kundaklanmak suretile yakıldı. O yanan evde Hit bedenen günlerce amele gibi çalıştı. Köyümüzün (150) senelik mazisi var. Bu yılların karşılığı üç yılda yapılanlar her yönden yüz elli yılda yapılmıslardan inanın çok fazladır. Son yaptımız örnek evden üç adet yapıldı. Köy için en büyük menfaat. Bu ev üzerinde düşünülürse, manası milli servet yönünden çok değerli olduğu anlaşılır kanatındayım. Hit (16) ay oldu köyümüze geleli, bu arada Barış Gönüllüleri Müdürü köyümüze geldiğinde yapılanları öğünerek anlatmıştık. Geçenlerde bir Müdür muavini ile birisi geldi. Ganatıma gore onun Türkçe bilmeyişi, durumu yanlış anlamasına sebeb olmuş buna köycek üzüldük. Biz Hitten köycek çok memnunuz. Bu Yazıları üzüntümüzü belirt etmek için en derin hislerimizle yaziyorum. Burada köyümün sizlere karşı sevgi ve saygılarını belirt eder hürmetgârlığımın iblağını rica ederim.

Bereketli Köyü Muhtarı
Kâmil Aslantekin

Yukarıda isimleri ile imzaları bulunan şahısların köyümüz hane reyisi oldukları ile imzalarığ kendilerine ayit olduğunu tastık ederim.

Bereketli Köyü M[uhtar]
[K Ö Y   M Ü H Ü R Ü]
KÂMİL ASLANTEKİN

30-1-1966
Bereketli Köyü

Barış gönüllüleri Müdürlüğüne

Ankara

Ben Balıkesir Vilayetine (25) Kilometre mesafede Kepekpınar Nahiyesinin Bereketli Köyü Muhtarı Kâmil Aslantekinim. İnkılâpta öğretmenden Muhtarlık Vazifesini Köyümün yüzde yüz isteğiyle Muhtar oldum. ve yine seçime iştirak halkın isteğiyle girüp yüzde (80) farkla Muhtar seçildim. Türkiyede Muhtarlık Vazifesi menfaat yönünden en bir ailenin (100) de üç ihtiyacı sağlanmaz. yalnız Muhtarlık Vazifesi hal miş bir Memleketin öz evlâdı olarak. Köyümün Maddi ve manevi ihtiyaçları içinde çırpınırken Amerikan Devletininin Nimetlerinden Devlet namı altında yardımlar yapıldığını bili yorduk. Fakat Amerikalıların ...kadar Mütevazı ve hürmetgâr aynı zamanda bilirsiz bir insan olduklarını ...bile kabul edeceği bir iş değildir. işte bu yazdığım misallerin hakikat ...duğunu hikim hareketleri ile anladık. ve Köylülerimiz arasında bir Amerikan ...illetinin nekadar iyi bir millet olduğu takdirle karşılandı. işte bu aralarda ... Bana yeni Köyümüze gelmiş idi. yalnız hepimizin malûmu türkçe bilmi ...larda bu arada Kayde bir doğum yüzünden zehirlenme vakası oldu ... Mehmet Sadık öz kanın ailesi Kekik yağı içmek suretile zehirlenmiş idi ... Köyde bütün ahalısı olduğu halde açık arabada bir kırak türkle bütün ... sırtından çıkardığı palto ile örtünmek suretile o soğuk havada hiç kendi ... sıhhatini düşünmeden Balıkesire doktora götürdü bu hareketi türk Köylü ... sunu inanın ağlattı. Kayde Kimde bir testavi edilecek yara kesik ... olursa olsun + gönülsüz hastaların evine gidip onları tedavi etti ... sağlık yönünden bukadar yazdığım bence kafi. 2- Hit bu aralar ... la bu Köy heyet odasında duruyorduk biz de onun fikirlerinden istifa ... ediyorduk. birgün Kavak ekme mevzuunu bize anlattı. ve biz de

-193-

anun fikrinden istifade etmek suretile *** Balıkesir yolu
üzerine (400) adet yeni tip kavak ektik. bu arada köyümüzde vaiz
Hocamız vardı. yirminci asırdan bas ediyorda dini yönden *** bir fid..
yetiştirmek, çok sevap olduğunu söyleyen Hocalarımız tenezzül edip kavak
ekmeye gelmediler. hiç enaz otuz kavak ektim. ve misal olarak
hiç köylülere gösterdim. Bu Memleket lâzım bir amerikalı *** Her
yönden çalta gösteriyorda bizler neden çalışmıyoruz dedim. çeşmeler
de selze ve beş yıkanıyorda. bunu da anun fikri ile çarak ettik.
ayrıca Köye örnek bir okulumuz önüne ev yaptık anunda yapılması..
Hitin çok rütü oldu. ayrıca Köy kahvesinin yanına bir havuz yapıldı.
Netice imece suretile yapılan her Köy işinde de hiç örnek misaller ve
**** Kerabpınar nahiye Müdürü ile Kumluyadık köyüne Kepsü yardımına gittik
rada Hit en yüksek yardımda bulundu. bu hal Nahiye Müdürünü ağla..
Netice iyi bary ile anlatmak la tükenmez. son olarak köyümüzde bir
angın hadisesi oldu. çelebili bir şahsın evi kundaktan mak suretile yakıldı..
ganan evde hiç bedenen günlerce amele gibi çalıştı. Köyümüzün (150) senelik
ozisi var. bu yılların karşı bize üç yılda yapılanlar her yönden yüz elli
lda yapılmışlardan inanın çok fazladır. son yaptığımız örnek evden üç
elli servet yönünden çok değerli olduğu anlaşılır Kanatındayım - Hitin
) ay oldu Köyümüze geldi. bu arada Barış gönüllüleri Müdürü Köyünüze geldiğinde
pılanları öğürerek anlatmıştık. geçenlerde bir Müdür muavini ile bisisi geld..
matıma göre anun türkçe bilmeyişi durumu ve yanlış anlamasına *** **
**** olmuş buna Köyçek üzüldük. Biz hitten Köyçek çak memnunuz.
yazaları üzün tümüzü belirt etmek için sizlere karşı sevgi ve
leri miz le yazıyorum - Burada Köyümün sizlere karşı sevgi ve
uygularını belirt eder hürmet gâr lığımın *** Lâğanı rica ederim.

Berghell ***
MH*** Kemal Pekintek

1 Nazım çakan
2 muhterem dilmaç
3 m sadık Dilek
4 Kerametin dilek
5 Ayhan hangül
6 m.sadık Demirel
7 ibrahim dilek
8 mehmet savaş
9 Recep Bergahan
10 m Ali Kaygı
11 Necdet can
12 ilhami Duman
13 Niyazi koç
14 Halil ergün
15 Celil ilhan
16 Sadetdin cengiz
17 ibrahim esender
18 fikret yılmaz
19 Baki yılmaz
20 Necip Can
21 Hakk Balcan
22 Sabri yılmaz
23 Adil balgün
24 Özcan çakan
25 Halitdin Cengiz
26 memet demiraş
27 vesat hazanap
28 Ahmet AlP.
29 şaban özdemir
30 Hüseyin Balcan
31 ilhan vedat

37 Adem deminalp
74 Süleyman Oagdelen
35 Amet ilhan
76 feyzi dursun
37 ibrahim Kandemir
37 Hasan dilmaç
39 isak cengiz
40 Sadatdin Ata

41 Nadi er

42 Bayram Ata
43 Orhan Dimiralp
44 idris Kayahan
45 Hakki ilhan
46 Orhan yılmaz
47 Sami Dilek
48 mehmet Demiralp
49 m.sadık Çakmak
50 ibrahim gelenbevi
51 Buran can
52 erdogan Can
53 idris Dilek

54 M.Ali ersoy
55 Cahit Cengiz
56 Şayir Aplay

57 yusuf ilhan

58 Halil Alo

59	Recep Dağdelen
60	Süleyman Çakır
61	Selahdin Dilmaç
62	Süleyman Aplay
63	M. Sadık Gözhan
64	Kemal İlhan
65	Mehmet Karaaslan
66	Ahmet Bozanalp
67	Halil Çetin
68	İdris İlhan
69	Hilmi Konmaz
70	M. Ali Balgün
71	Servet Doğankan
72	Eyüp Hayat
73	İsmail Alınmış
74	İsmail Baltaş
75	Rıza Demiralp
76	İdris Kaydınıra
77	Şakir Durdu
78	İbrahim Dolu
79	Mustafa Gezer
80	Recep Balgün
81	H. Hüseyin Dilek
82	İsmail Balgün
83	Hüseyin Karaman

85	Turan Arp
86	Turgut irkil
87	~~Hay~~ Ahmet Duman
88	Avni erdem
89	Ali Dilmaç
90	ismail Kayğa
91	ilhami er
92	Davut ilhan
93	ibrahim Koç
94	Hasan özdemir
95	Ersin demirel
96	ünal ilhan
97	irfan dilmaç
98	Serai Duman
99	M. Sadik Dogantekin
100	yüksel Koç
101	Enver erdoğan
102	Hayri Aslantekin
103	Hasan Bayat
104	tahsin Demirtaş
105	mustafa Koç
106	ibrahim Ata
107	Bedritdin can b
108	özet Dogantekin
109	Arif Aslantekin
110	vahit erdoğan

112   Musa Er —
113   Ali Gezer
114   Kamil Bacak
115   ümmet doğantekin ÜRÖVÖRÖTEKIN
116   ismail Can
117   Emin Demirkol
118   Hüseyin Boğanalp
119   Hasan hüseyin
120   Bedirit din cengiz
121   Muamber erden
122   Cemal dilek
123   mehmet balcan
124   Kamil Doğantekin
125   mehmet can
126   Mustafa Doğantekin
127   Sedat Demirel S. Demirel
128   Halit çakan HALIT ÇAKAN

yukarıda isimleri ve imzaları Bulunan
ların köyümüz Hane reisi oldukları ve
imzalarığ kendilerine agit olduğunu Tas...
e de rim.
Berefetli Köyü

Kâmil aslan teli